SHATTERED
BY ONE'S TOUCH
AND WE OVERCAME

FOREWORD BY DR. JUANITA WOODSON

SHATTERED
BY ONE'S TOUCH
AND WE OVERCAME

VISIONARY AUTHOR

MARCELINE WILLIAMS

Disclaimer

This book contains content intended for mature readers. Within its pages are scenes and themes of an explicit and graphic nature that some readers may find disturbing or offensive. Such content may include, but is not limited to, strong language, sexual scenes, violence, and sensitive subject matter.

Reader discretion is strongly advised. The author and publisher make no representation concerning the suitability of this content for any particular audience. By continuing beyond this page, you acknowledge and accept that you are reading this material of your own free will and at your own risk.

Persons under the age of 18, or the applicable age of majority in their jurisdiction, should not proceed without the consent of a parent or guardian.

CONTENTS

Dedicated to the only
Deliverer, Sustainer,
Healer and Protector
The Lord Jesus Christ

FOREWORD

Celebrating the Voices of Women

In a world that is constantly evolving, it's without hesitation to acknowledge and honor the diverse and profound contributions made by women who impact the world and the lives of so many others. Their stories, experiences, and perspectives have shaped societies, broken barriers, and will continue to inspire future generations and world leaders. This anthology stands as a testament to the extraordinary power and resilience of women across the globe.

Within these pages, you will encounter a kaleidoscope of narratives, each one a unique expression of the myriad of journeys women embark upon in pursuit of their dreams and aspirations. From the unyielding strength of mothers and caregivers to trailblazing pioneers who shattered glass ceilings, from professionals whose passion illuminates what it means to be a woman to caregivers fighting for their families, this collection encompasses a tapestry of voices that harmonize to tell powerful stories of womanhood.

At the heart of these stories lies the indomitable spirit of perseverance that has fueled the women who faced adversity, discrimination, abuse, financial struggle, and other seemingly insurmountable challenges. Their experiences have demonstrated time and time again that courage, determination, and solidarity can overcome any obstacle. This is a prime example of how painful experiences can serve as fuel, catapulting them to the soaring heights of success they have realized and continuously shaping who they are today.

As we turn the pages of this anthology, we must remember that the struggles faced by women are not isolated, but represent their truth and triumphs. The voices you will encounter resonate not just with women but with humanity as a whole. In each narrative, we find God's jewels speaking with strength and assertiveness. We also find threads of hope, unity, dignity, pride, and a shared vision for a more inclusive, compassionate, and equitable world.

While recognizing their accomplishments and struggles of the past, we must also acknowledge the God-breathed future that awaits all women through these encouraging and powerful words of wisdom. They also speak to the coming generations, who will prayerfully inherit a world where every woman is free to express her voice, pursue dreams without fear, abuse, hatred, or prejudice.

To the authors whose words grace these pages, I extend my deepest prayers for their depth, courage, and brevity in sharing their stories and experiences. Just their courage alone in opening up their fragile hearts and lives will undoubtedly inspire readers to explore their own untold testimonies. We must applaud the profound impact of these women's contributions to our lives.

To the readers, I invite you to immerse yourselves in this literary voyage, to listen intently to the diverse voices of women, and I pray that you gain a deeper appreciation for the immeasurable value they bring to the tapestry of womanhood.

I celebrate the resilience, intelligence, and grace of all women. It takes grace to stand through the fire and come out as pure gold. Only a God can do that. There's beauty for ashes in every story.

Let's all be inspired by their stories. It takes working together and sharing together to create a world where every woman's potential is birthed at the proper time and knows no boundaries. When we keep God in His rightful place in our lives (hopefully He's always somewhere right in the center), we know that healing, radical change, deliverance, and miracles are inevitable.

With utmost admiration and respect for the women who continue to shape our future and our world,

Dr. Juanita Woodson

INTRODUCTION

Woman, the courage to be vulnerable pass the childhood trauma and chaos is definitely a battle of the spoken word concerning destiny. Think about it, what is something that one has tried to forget, held captive in the rear of the mind, or in the depths of the dormant space? For years we as <u>Grown</u> and <u>Sexy</u> women have flawlessly become a bright light through pain and disappointment from the hidden aroma of sex.

Absolutely, rather good or inevitably bad. Obtainable by one's choice is good, right? Well in the life of a Believer that's only for the married, and it should be good, great or grander between Man and Woman. Shattering components of women's life stories of desiring healthy, whole and the best relationships of their lives with partners, parents, siblings and children are the most compassionate and authentic stories you will digest. Look into the deep level of trauma some of these ladies encountered and then look at their **boldness of overcoming** fear. As said by Oprah Winfrey, *"The great courageous act that we must all do, is to have the courage to step out of our history and past so that we can live our dreams.*

As these fallible stories about overcoming Habits and Addictions, Controlling Relationships, Incest, Rape and Molestation, Teen Pregnancy and more captures your heart and pulls you in, when you see yourself, just **breathe** and **let go**.

Dreams are real and happiness is peaceful, praying for wealth and peace for your breakthrough today and forever. Memphis Bold, Brave and Brilliant Tears Blossom Collection Volume I.

Shattered by One's Touch and We Overcame.

SHATTERED BY ONE'S TOUCH
FROM DEFEAT TO DESTINY

MARQUIEPTA ODOM-WILLIAMS

Marquiepta Odom-Williams serves as the Executive Director of YWCA Greater Memphis, an organization primarily focused on providing shelter and resources for domestic violence victims. As a teenager, Marquiepta witnessed domestic violence within her own home and later became a victim herself in her early twenties.

Today, she stands as a triumphant survivor, empowering individuals to attain self-sufficiency, transcend past traumas, and discover a purpose beyond their pain as she aids in reconstructing their lives.

Marquiepta holds a Bachelor of Science in Management and Organizational Development from Bethel University. She is a graduate of the Leading-Up Leadership Program, sponsored by Momentum Non-Profit Partners, and the Tommie Burks Academy. Additionally, she holds a comprehensive specialist certification in domestic violence, sexual assault, and program specialization from the National Advocate Credentialing Program (NACP).

In addition to her role as Executive Director, Marquiepta takes on various community roles. She is an ordained minister, motivational speaker, and teacher, often referred to as "the quiet storm" and "secret agent" because of her unique delivery style. She communicates messages of hope, help, and healing to women and is the founder of GOWAC Ministry (Giving Our Women A Chance). She frequently appears on WAVE TREND and is a former co-host of the radio show "Let's Talk About". Marquiepta mentors teen girls and women, and serves as an Advisory Board Member for the Shelby County Community Service Agency. She is also an Advisory Committee Member of 'You Have the Power' for West Tennessee, and 'Wrap Around Shelby'. Her additional service roles include the Shelby County Social Services and Health Committee, the State of Tennessee Shelter Advisory Committee, the State of Tennessee STOP Advisory Committee team, the Visible Music College Women In Leadership Advisory Committee, and the District Attorney's Office Community Justice Program. She is a former board member for YLove and Memphis Shelby County Domestic and Sexual Violence Council.

Marquiepta's mission is to assist those who have been victimized, helping them heal and pursue their destinies.

SHATTERED BY ONE'S TOUCH FROM DEFEAT TO DESTINY

Life can take us on a journey full of obstacles and teachable moments. In many cases, all we can think about is the unfairness of the circumstances and wonder if the bad seasons will soon end. Dreadful things can occur and as a result, our innocence can be taken away at an early age or in adulthood. These life-changing events can be so unexpected that it only takes one traumatizing experience to change a child's perspective of the world, family, and themselves.

We tend to live our lives based on personal experiences and learned behavior, which often originate within the home. It is sad to say, but families often overlook problems within the home and choose not to address them. The root of the problem is within the heart and mind of adults in the home. Unaddressed family problems and secrets can cause <u>trauma</u> and <u>adverse childhood experiences</u> in children residing in the home. Adverse childhood experiences can last a lifetime. Therefore, it is crucial for adults to remember that any life-altering event a child experiences or witnesses in the home can result in the child experiencing adverse childhood experiences.

The hurt is real for so many individuals, and the damage may last a lifetime if there is no accountability and removal of the offender from the home. It is essential for someone in the home to speak up. When another adult is aware of the issues in the home and chooses not to speak up, it causes the victim to trust no one. Staying quiet when someone is in danger in the home is a real issue, and it is commonly referred to as "Home with the Hush Factor" (HWTHF). This term represents the silence, refusal to confront and address the dreadful sins of intimate partner violence, molestation, child abuse, neglect, trauma, addictions, and other related issues that are unfortunately kept hidden.

When there is <u>trauma</u> there are also <u>triggers</u>. I called them the two T's. The two T's can last a lifetime if we do not recognize and seek godly and/or therapeutic counseling. The two Ts of Trauma and Triggers are real and can leave a lasting effect if we do not receive the proper care. This story is about a little girl who struggled from childhood to early adulthood because of trauma and triggers she experienced from an early age.

Sapphire was a playful and happy little girl. She grew up in a middle-class family and from the outside looking in, it appeared that she was living her best life. People often thought of her family as the rich ones on the street, and a notable example for other families. Just like other families, her household had numerous dysfunctions and faced many struggles. Sapphire did not know her father was an alcoholic because she was too young to understand. I guess Sapphire's family had learned to mask their issues from the outside world. And yes, they did an incredibly excellent job of it.

During the early years of Sapphire's life everything was going well. Her father was her everything. She was daddy's little girl. All she talked about was her dad. She often asked him to bring the big 18-wheeler home from work. Her dad often granted her request and stopped by their home on his way out of town. This gave her a chance to show her friends the big truck her daddy drove while at work. He would blow the truck horn and allow the other children to sit in the cab of the 18-wheeler. The children in the neighborhood admired the truck and were excited to see him drive through.

Every child expects and desires *love, protection*, *guidance*, and *provision* in their home. The saying home is where the heart is can be overrated because the heart is often broken and a child cannot register home as a safe place, but one of torment and fear. Just like that, one night Sapphire's child-like innocence was taken away from her. No, her father did not molest her. He was very respectful regarding her space and being a female. The night she heard her parents fighting for the first time was life changing. She ran into the room to witness her father pinning her mother down and hitting her. She was so frightened by the scene in her parents' bedroom because she had never witnessed or heard her parents fight or argue in the past. She immediately ran to the front door to get help, but her intoxicated father rushed behind her as she attempted to get out of the house and get help for her mother. Her father hit, pushed, and dared her to go out the door.

Sapphire did not have any visible physical injuries, but the internal heartbreak was killing her. Can you imagine a young pre-teen broken by the one man she loved the most? In that moment Sapphire's life changed forever. This incident also changed her view of her father and men. He went from being her hero to the person she secretly despised the most. This was her first experience with trauma, and the beginning of her developing triggers. This was also the beginning of her spiraling out of control, but she was young so no one could tell. The two Ts of triggers and trauma would follow her for over 30 years.

Of course, no one knew about the incident that occurred because their home was now the home with the hush factor (HWTHF). Her mother left her father immediately after the incident, but because of the hush factor, no one knew what really occurred that night. She was sworn to secrecy by her mother to never tell anyone. That was a lot for a small brain to carry and her heart and soul were broken. Sapphire and her mother stayed away for about six months. Her father asked her mother to forgive him, and he pleaded with her for them to return home. After several meetings and her father apologizing, they returned home. Although the family was reunited, it was no longer her place of security. She no longer felt the love she once felt. The place Sapphire used to call home sweet home had become a shadowy and sad place.

She could not understand why the incident occurred. There were nights when she cried herself to sleep because she thought she caused her father to hit her. Sapphire just could not understand why the man that took her everywhere with him when he was off work would cause her so much pain. She was broken, bruised, and was mentally damaged, but no one knew how she really felt. At an early age she learned to live her life with masks on. If someone had taken the time to look in her eyes, they would have known Sapphire needed help. She was sinking into a dark place yet smiling all the time. The brokenness caused her to develop the wrong image of herself. She no longer loved herself and thought she was too short, too skinny, not smart enough, and she learned to avoid mirrors as much as possible.

Sapphire's grandmother was a strong woman and believed in prayer. She would often tell her that she was loved and that she would do great things in life. She loved her grandmother and held on to every word her granny spoke into her life. She often took Sapphire to church and prayer meetings. Despite all the chaos in her life she would hold on to and think of the conversations she often had with her grandmother. She spent as much time as she could with her granny. She loved to talk with her because she believed her granny was her guardian angel. Sapphire also believed that her grandmother could just look at her and feel her pain. She would look her in the eyes and tell her, I know you have some deep hurt and things going on, but just know all of this will work for your good. During many of those hard times in life she would hear her grandmother's voice. She imparted wisdom in her and would often tell her that she would be a change agent one day for women and teens.

Although she dedicated her life to Christ early, that did not change the path she was on. Deep in her heart she held onto the things her granny instilled in her. Because of her brokenness, it seemed as if every area of her life was affected by the trauma. Deep inside she had a secret hatred for her mom for returning to her father.

Sapphire only thought about her dad hitting and hurting her. She believed that was why her mom should not have returned home. She wanted to write her mother a letter or hold a sign up to remind her that, "mommy, he hurt your baby girl." In Sapphire's heart and mind that was enough to cause them to never return home.

She believed her mother should have protected her by not returning to the home of the person that hurt her baby. She did not realize at the time that her mother assumed that she was okay. She often continued with her life and responded to Sapphire as if the incident did not affect her. It was hard for her to understand her mother's behavior.

As Sapphire became older, she also became more withdrawn, and had limited communication with her mother. It is hard to imagine that this teen lived in the home but had limited conversations with her mother. She often acted out because there were a number of situations that occurred in her life that triggered her.

Sapphire was often labeled as the child that was spoiled and often seemed troubled. No one realized that the trauma caused all her issues. She could not tell her mother how she felt regarding her emotions, fears, pains, low self-esteem, feeling unwanted and unloved, and often thought about committing suicide. Because of their communication issues, her relationship with her mother became very unhealthy. Sapphire often recalled how communication with her mother became so bad. As a result, she did not receive the reassurance she needed from her mother, and she thought her mother did not love her. Sapphire could count on one hand how often her mother told her she loved her after the incident that dreary night. Validation and love are so important to any child growing up. Sapphire was no different than any other child seeking love and validation.

There was no way she could tell her mother how she really felt. Because of the strain on their relationship, she could not receive the counseling she really needed. It did not occur to her that her mother needed counseling and help also. In their culture the hush factor outweighed seeking the help needed to improve mental health and family relationships.

The love that she once shared with her father suddenly turned into pain. This pain continued to follow her for many years from her teens, well into adulthood. As a teen she thought she was ready to love, but she was nowhere near ready. Sapphire was longing for the love she once shared with her father. This caused her to look for love in all the wrong places. She really did not understand what love was.

Sapphire was looking for a man to replace the love she lost that night at an early age. She ended up in so many relationships as a teen. She often dated without her parents knowing. Each time she would end up being hurt and lonely. Sapphire developed a pattern of listening to the words I love you, only to be misused and abused. She thought the behavior was normal because of the night her dearly beloved father hit her. She thought it was because of her shape, her hair, her this or that, but truly it was because she was too young to love. It was because she was scared and bruised internally. It manifested externally as she needed love. She was willing to do anything to relive that feeling she once had with her father. Just like an addict, she was game for whatever to feel that way again. She was always drawn to older men because she was looking for the validation of a father's love but did not understand what was going on inside of her. Validation from a father is so important. Fathers should be the first men to show and teach their daughters what to expect, accept, and behavior not to expect or accept from a man in a dating relationship or marriage. In her mind her father did not love her, but she did not understand he really loved her. The trauma from the one-time abuse led her to believe that he hated her. When he tried to get close to her the trauma would trigger her. She would close her heart towards her dad.

And just like that, Sapphire found herself in a relationship with a 23-year-old man and she was only sixteen. She lied to her mother to meet him one night and he raped her. She was too afraid to tell anyone because she had lied to her mom. She did not even tell her best friend. The guy would not answer her calls after that night. Once again, Sapphire was broken, felt dirty, and fell deeper into depression and self-hatred was getting stronger each day, but no one knew. She felt rejected, lonely, and ugly, but she kept her mask on. She was not happy at all although she had good grades in school, was a flag girl and majorette. Repeatedly she would end up in bad relationships with verbal abuse. One day at the age of seventeen, she took a bottle of Tylenol to end her life, but her attempt was unsuccessful. She recovered from the incident but did not receive any real intervention. God would not allow her the easy way out. She had an assignment that she would fulfill years later.

As a young adult, she continued looking for love in wrong places. Time after time she ended up dating men who were just like her father. This occurred numerous times and did not end until she sought counseling many years later. Men, be very careful how you treat your daughters because when she starts dating, she will most likely end up dating someone just like you. Will that be a good or a bad decision for her?

At the age of twenty-four Sapphire thought she had met the one. She was right, he was the one, but not the one God sent for her. He was a chameleon with lots of charm and was very charismatic. It was amazing how he knew exactly what to say to her. Sapphire could not resist his choice of words and boy was he handsome.

She thought her prince charming had found her, but little did she know it was just the opposite. She was so ready to move out of her parents' home that she was almost willing to do whatever. Because of her low self-esteem it never crossed her mind that she could move out on her own and start her life. She did not know about Section 8 or any other housing assistance programs at the time.

Sapphire thought getting married would be her door to freedom from her parents' home. She had no idea that her Prince charming was a broken man that was hurt. We all know the results of dating a hurt person. Hurt people only hurt those they should love the most. Just like so many other women she did not notice the red flags or she may have decided to ignore them. When an abuser reveals who they are it is important to pay attention and make quality decisions regarding the situation. The victim/survivor must have the strength and gain the knowledge they need to understand they are in an abusive intimate partner relationship. Taking back their own power is so important. It is sad to say, but Sapphire just did not have the tools she needed to understand the red flags.

The relationship started off surprisingly good, but after a few months she caught him cheating. Of course, he convinced her that it was not true. She desperately wanted to believe him because she was lonely and broken. Her current state of mind led her to go with the flow despite the pain she was experiencing. The trauma she experienced throughout the years led her heart instead of good judgment leading her. The trauma she had dealt with since pre-teen was still affecting her and was a part of her decision making. She allowed him to insult her by not correcting his behavior. She felt if she just acted the way he wanted the relationship would be okay. She did not understand the more she surrendered to his insults, manipulating and controlling behavior the worst it would get. Sapphire also thought that she could change him. He had to make the decision that he wanted to change, but he thought he was okay. He did not think he needed counseling because he was a man, and that is how he was supposed to behave and respond. He had a lot of trauma and was acting out because of the effects of his adverse childhood experiences.

Needless to say, he convinced her to stay. She was very smart with book sense, but street sense was another story. Sapphire had a rocky relationship with this guy, but again she wanted to move out of her parents' home so badly that she accepted his behavior. He did not hit her, at least not in the beginning, but he did not treat her as if he loved her. Verbal abuse is still a form of intimate partner domestic violence.

People say that words cannot hurt us, but hearing negative words over and over does affect us. He asked her to marry him, and she did. They went to the courthouse and got married. This was the beginning of the end. In less than a month he was cheating and often did not come home. He would call her names and belittle her. One day they were arguing, and he hit her. He would yell, scream, and use intimidation to frighten her. She suffered and survived so many brutal beatings at the hands of the man who claimed he loved her. One night in particular they were driving home. He started an argument and she spoke up. He backhanded her, breaking her nose. Blood flowed all over her clothes. After his explosion of anger, he would be nice and calm and would often give her beautiful gifts, pay for a spa day, and a salon day. Just like any other typical abuser, he would often beg, plead, and promise not to do it again. He would also use the typical phase, I do not know what came over me, it was my bad day at work. This is called the honeymoon phase. This is normal behavior after a violent explosion.

The breaking of her nose ended up being the final one for Sapphire, she was tired. She started praying and asking God to deliver her. Her grandmother continued to intercede for her. She knew something was not right but would only tell her granddaughter she was praying for her. Remember Sapphire grew up as a Christian, but over time the trauma, triggers, and wanting to live her life as she chose, she turned from the source of her help. The more she prayed it seemed like the abuse and her life in general was spiraling out of control.

No one can predict when a woman has taken all she can stand. It is sad to say that if she does not get out of the violent relationship, she could become a fatality. This often occurs when she feels as if she has no way out. On the other hand, when enough becomes too much and a victim of intimate partner violence is tired, that person may choose to take matters in her own hands. Just like that, one night Sapphire snapped and decided to kill her husband in his sleep. She was desperate and just could not see a way out, and no one in her family knew what was going on. All her issues including the effects of adverse childhood experience had caught up with her. The lifelong journey of untreated and undiagnosed trauma and triggers had finally manifested their ugly heads in Sapphire. At that moment she did not recognize herself. Those unresolved issues that she did not deal with were now controlling Sapphire. Her husband had no idea that arguing and hitting her a few hours earlier would possibly lead to his death. She had turned into another person, a person who had snapped as she planned her husband's demise. She loaded the gun and waited until he went to sleep. Once he was sound asleep, she got across his body and put the gun to his head. She woke him up and he was terrified. He told her she was crazy, and quickly begged for his life. The calm and easy-going Sapphire was no longer there. She had spaced out and decided to play "Russian Roulette" with him. She pulled the trigger the first time, but it was not a live round. He was crying and used the bathroom on himself. He told her she was crazy again and she said "yes, you made me this way." She pulled the trigger again, but still no live round. Remember she had a praying grandmother. By this time, a cool breeze calm came over Sapphire and she snapped out of the trance. She did not have a clue as to what had just happened. She got off her husband and immediately he grabbed his keys and fled their home in the condition he was in with no pants and only soiled underwear.

She examined the gun and realized that if she would have pulled the trigger a third time, she would have committed murder by killing her husband. At that point she realized she needed help, and she had to get out of the marriage. This was the beginning of Sapphire's deliverance. She cried and began to thank God for allowing her not to pull the trigger a third time. She knew deep inside that her praying grandmother and the Holy Spirit saved her early that morning.

She realized that she had some unresolved issues dating back many years. She did not know it was trauma. She did not realize that she was often triggered by certain foods, smells, words, touch, sex, gestures etc., but she knew something was wrong with her. Sapphire did not realize that as an adult she was paralyzed by adverse childhood experiences. She knew that it was time to call her Pastor, get back in fellowship with the body of Christ and rededicate her life back to God. She fell on her knees and began to thank God for freedom. Later that day, she had the locks changed on the doors. She contacted a divorce attorney to start the divorce process. She scheduled an appointment to meet with her Pastor and wife. She also made an appointment for her first counseling session.

As in a typical intimate partner domestic violence situation, most of her family and friends did not know what she was going through. They had no idea she was in an intimate partner domestic violence relationship. She would stay away from those who loved her when she had physical signs of abuse on her body. She had also learned to mask her pains and emotions. Now, she was ready to fight to be free from everything that held her back. She was ready to learn to love herself and take her life back. Sapphire was determined to change her life. She was ready to move forward with her life and break this generational curse off her life. She saw her mother go through intimate partner domestic violence, and later in life, she found out her grandmother was also a victim of domestic violence. She was determined she would get her healing, therapy, and everything else she needed. She was ready to be the person she only dreamed of becoming. Sapphire was ready to be the person her grandmother decreed and declared she would be.

Sapphire reunited and surrounded herself with people who loved her. She released the shame and embarrassment and the notion of what people thought of her. She completed her counseling classes, she divorced her husband, she reunited with the church, and became faithful. Was it easy? No, but she was determined to fight for a better Sapphire. In the past, she fought for unhealthy relationships, to hate her parents, and she fought not to love herself. At that moment in time, she finally felt beautiful, empowered, and ready for the next chapter in her life. She was not ready to date yet because she wanted to date herself and understand who she was. She forgave her parents because she realized that they were dealing with their own undiagnosed trauma, and they both had triggers from the issues they experienced growing up. She did not give them a pass for the trauma they caused her, but she did let it go. She even forgave all those who abused her, including the one who raped her, as well as her ex-husband. No, it was not easy, but with a village surrounding her, including her parents, she was able to move forward. She was able to break the generational curse of abuse off her bloodline. Her granny was still her biggest cheerleader, imparting in her and preparing her for greater things.

Today, Sapphire is thriving and making a profound impact on the world around her. She empowers other women; she serves as a mentor, a friend, a wife, a mother – fierce, loving, healed, and a Boss. Above all, she loves God and cherishes her life. Sapphire firmly believes that everything she went through was essential. She reaches out to women in pain, helping them heal from their trauma and triggers because she has not only lived through it but grown through it. She understands that every person's story is unique, but she holds the belief that purpose can emerge from pain. She even returned to college and successfully graduated. Sapphire stands as an authentic example that our past experiences do not dictate who we are meant to become.

From the very moment of conception, a purpose is assigned to us. Satan glimpses who we are meant to be, and without delay, he sets out to thwart us. The magnitude of the task determines the intensity of the trials and tribulations we face. Often, these challenges commence early in life to obstruct us from fully embracing our destiny. Each of us must live our lives deliberately and intentionally, bearing in mind that to catalyze change, we must be change agents! Sapphire embodied this principle and emerged as a true champion. And to you, the reader, know this: YOU ARE DESTINED TO CHANGE THE WORLD!

STANDING AGAINST ALL ODDS

MELBA GILMORE-COLE

I am the biological mother of six children, and I also have three stepchildren from my current husband. As a teacher, I have chosen to homeschool my youngest child through the "Gateway Home Schooling Program." I was born in Forest City, Arkansas, but I spent most of my childhood in Cleveland, Ohio. Currently, I reside in Memphis, Tennessee, where I have decided to raise my children.

My journey to deepen my relationship with Christ and grow in Him led me to become a member of The Pursuit of God Transformation Center. Where I also teach youth between the ages of 2 to 11. Additionally, I serve as a member of the Prayer Team and the Evangelism Team. Also, I attend the Bible College, Life Christian University.

In addition to being a wife and a mother, I am actively involved in business. I manage my time by joining my husband as a marketer of LegalShield. I am also a licensed Childcare Specialist.

Life in this earthly realm has presented its share of hardships, challenges, and pain. However, I firmly believe in the strength of women. Above all, I find my ultimate strength and joy in the Lord.

"I can do all things through Christ who strengthens me."
(Philippians 4:13)

STANDING AGAINST ALL ODDS

They say, "What doesn't kill you makes you stronger." I know this is a bit cliché, but I can't find a better phrase that captures the essence of the story I'm about to share. This is the story of a lost, scared little girl navigating her way through the maze of life. It speaks of her triumphs and trials, joys and sorrows, and moments that were either deeply devastating or unbelievably peaceful. As she fumbled through her journey to adulthood, she learned some tough lessons. These lessons did one of two things—they either became experiences that led to wisdom, or they quieted that intuitive voice within her that deciphered "right" from "wrong". This lost and frightened little girl was me.

When I first agreed to share my story, I knew that I would have to relive some very painful parts of my life, but I quickly brushed this thought aside. Instead, I focused on the "why"—why I needed to tell my story. I wanted to share because I hoped that my story could help someone else find their voice, to stand up and speak out, or to persist in asking for help until someone responds. But, when I sat down to put my thoughts on paper, that very thought I had dismissed suddenly confronted me, causing a whirlwind of emotions. I found myself in a whirl of emotional **"highs"** and **"lows"**. Some memories were buried deep in the past, but they were still so vivid that I didn't have to dig too deep to remember the emotions or trauma I had experienced. Like anyone else, these are memories I wish I could forget. Yet, there were also some happy memories that were somewhat dimmed by the negative ones. For these, I had to focus and carefully piece them together. The one thing I realized while walking down memory lane was that in one way or another, God was always there ensuring that I emerged victorious in the end. It's interesting how human memory works, isn't it?

Memories can be sparked by anything, from a pleasant aroma to a catchy commercial jingle, or even a movie where the protagonist's story mirrors our own. Occasionally, one memory might prompt another, meaning a delightful memory could lead to a less pleasant one. I refer to this as going down the 'rabbit hole'.

Within that hole, we start linking one recollection to the next. For instance, when I think of my mother, I remember her doing her utmost to care for my siblings and me. We weren't affluent, but we had a roof over our heads and, mostly, we had what we needed. Although initially reflecting on my mother brings back the fondness of a happy childhood during a time when I believed we were 'making it', this single tender thought often segues into a recollection of not truly feeling loved by her despite being cared for. In fact, I'm not entirely certain she knew how to love us. Reflecting now, I wonder if she couldn't love us because she wasn't taught how to. Contemplating that possibility, I'm torn between feeling pity or resentment. Should I sympathize with her struggle or feel angry that she wasn't inspired to do better, to give more than what she received for our sake? See, a roller coaster of emotions and we've only just started. Regardless, I'm immensely appreciative of this opportunity to share all my ups and downs, highs and lows, raw wounds and healed scars if it may aid others.

Here we go . . . .

Starting from the beginning, I was born January 18,1968 to Gloria J. Burnom and Lawrence Freeman. My father was not really involved in my life as I was growing up. Well, at least I have no recollection of such a relationship. As a matter of fact, I was four or five years old when my mother told me that my father was dead, and because I didn't see him much, I had little choice but to believe her. Before my father was completely out of the picture, the most graphic memory that I have of my father is at the age of two and is not at all a fond one. Actually, it's not really a father/daughter memory at all. This memory only includes my father by association. When I was two years old, my father's friend molested me. Some researchers contend that children experience childhood amnesia and do not have memories from the age of three to four or that we remember very little before the age of seven. Others also believe that even recollecting something as traumatic as childhood sexual abuse can be difficult due to memory deficit or time disorientation. In other words, how we remember childhood events as an adult can be altered. I can't say that I fully disagree with these statements, but in this case, I do beg to differ. No, I do not have an eidetic memory (photographic memory) or perfect recollection, but this incident I can vividly recall.

On this day, my mother and I were at my grandmother's house. My father, along with his friend "Lee", came to pick up my mother for a day out. At this time, I was still potty trained, so "Lee" took me to the bathroom. As he was a friend, no one gave it much thought that he would do my parents this favor and help. As the old saying goes "it takes a village", right? In the bathroom "Lee" told me we were going to do something that was not going to hurt me. I remembered him grabbing the Vaseline and that which followed was immense and excruciating pain. My undeveloped two-year old body was violated and intruded upon; my trust and innocence completely betrayed. The pain did not end there and neither did my lack of understanding. My mother took me to the doctor where I underwent a thorough examination. My two-year old mind didn't really comprehend what was happening. I only knew that it hurt. Thankfully, "Lee" did not get away with what he did to me. After this incident, the already almost non-existent presence of my father became scarcer. Things became intensely strained between him and my mother. In retrospect, I wondered if this incident was my mother's motivation for "killing off" my father as mentioned earlier. I imagine at this point he was dead to her already, she just wanted me to emulate her sentiment. My mother also became more protective and would only allow me to be with other women when I could not be under her watchful eye. In thinking back and reminiscing over my life, other memories, albeit seemingly small but indeed significant to me becoming who I am today, began to surface. One such memory was when I received salvation. As early as I can remember, like many I'm sure, church was not as much a choice as it was a mandatory obligation in my home in Cleveland, Ohio. My mother had us in church at least three days out of the week. I imagine praising the Lord was the most important and deciding factor for my mother attending church, but I can't help but wonder if she too was acting according to muscle memory because that is just the way things were. Much like Joshua told the Israelites and their elders, heads, and judges at Shechem " . . . as for me and my household, we will serve the Lord." (The Living Bible), so regardless of whether it was by force or by choice, my mother was in church and therefore so were we. At the age of eight, I decided to give my life to Christ. I had to be there anyway, so why not. At the time, it seemed easy enough, but of course, divine purpose, being in service to the Church, or living for Christ were all foreign concepts to me. It would not be until much later that I truly understood what the Word of God says in 2 Timothy 1:9, *"It is He who saved us and chose us for His Holy work not because we deserved it up because that was His plan long before the world began-to show His love and kindness to us through Christ"* (The Living Bible).

Before I reached the point in my life that I truly understood what it meant to be a part of the body of Christ, trauma would find me again. At the age of 15, I would experience my choice to say "no" taken away from me again by my uncle, "Boris". I later found out that my mother too fell victim to sexual abuse from her uncles, so like a generational curse, it seemed like this type of misfortune was my only fortune growing up. Once again, I was at my grandmother's house asleep on the couch. I woke up to "Boris" already having sex with me. This time I felt total shame and guilt because I let it happen even though I still did not understand what was happening (even at the age of 15). I informed my family of what happened, but instead of empathy or sympathy, I received blame and harsh words. They took "Boris's" side. Having thought about it, I wonder how they perceived who I was to be able to cast such chastising, scornful, and stigmatizing words at me. That day I was "stoned" twice and both times came with a hard lesson. I learned that bad decisions did not always come with consequences and "choice" was only a six-letter word that for me escaped definition because I consistently did not have one. I could only live, love, and let go. I suppose I must appreciate the irony of this lesson because L-O-V-E was yet another word that I was oblivious to. I have never received it, nor did I have any idea of what it was. I asked myself all the stereotypical or commonplace questions.

So what is love? How do I love others? How do I know when others love me? Is love just an emotion and if so, what does it feel like? Can I love myself? How does that feel or present itself? I had so many questions but no answers. Feasibly, I had answers, but I could not or was unwilling to see them at the time. With my misguided past as my compass, I started to look for love in all the wrong places, people, and things. I was fully convinced of only two things; I did not receive love from my parents or anyone else in my life, and I needed to find it to feel whole.

While confusing up for down and vice versa, I failed to look at our greatest example, God. The Word of God in Romans 5:8 tells us that " . . . *God showed His great love for us by sending Christ to die for us while we were still sinners."* (The Living Bible). It is not that I wanted to neglect God's altruistic, unconditional love, I just really did not see God much in the situations that I was facing in my life.

Molested twice at this point, blamed for one, and feeling discarded by my family, I did not whole heartedly understand the love that God had for me, so I just did not take the time to get to know who He is. As I mentioned earlier, I started looking for love in everything and everyone but God. At the age of 16 I moved out of my grandmother's house. With no plans and no direction, I ran headfirst into a relationship with a man that I thought could teach me what love was. For the first time, I felt like I had a choice. I chose to give my body to this man. I then began to equate love with sex. However, he did not seem to show me attention or affection in any other capacity. Even though I was still unclear about what love was, I knew for sure that this was not it. By this time, I was a teenage mother. At 16, I gave birth to my eldest son. It's an age-old story that having children can change you.

Holding my son, caring for him, and being everything he needed me to be (and so I thought), I felt something I'd never experienced before.

Here I had this little person that depended on me for everything although I did not have much, and I could barely care for myself because I did not know how. Despite that, I was able to see my whole world in that little baby's face. In my mind, he would love me unconditionally and I could love him back. I latched on to that ray of hope that I'd finally felt loved by someone and started to look for love in having children. The more children I have the more people there are to love me, right?

Finally able to see some type of light at the end of my long and dreary tunnel, I was pulled back into hopelessness. At the age of 18, I was raped at gunpoint and forced to smoke crack cocaine for hours. I was living with a friend, and one night she asked me to go with her someplace. She was a friend of mine, so I did not approach the situation with much caution. I agreed to go out with her. Her boyfriend, "Jr.", would be our transportation. When I got into the car, "Jr." locked all the doors and drove off. I was afraid and alone with someone I did not know.

He continued to drive until we reached the Lamplighter Hotel. Then my world would be shattered again. He held me at gunpoint forcing me to perform sexual acts with no contraception and do drugs.

That nightmare finally ended when he left the room. Despite being terrified to say anything, due to my family not believing me in the past, the possibility of being in trouble because of the drugs, and that he could return at any moment, I mustered the courage to call room service and asked them to call the police. The police arrived, but "Jr." never came back. The police treated me with great compassion and understanding. They took their report and instructed me to go to a rape crisis clinic to receive a rape kit. Until this day I'm not sure if the rape kit was ever analyzed as the back log for such things can span years. There is a fact that I am confident and sure of. God kept my mind and my body despite my life's devastations. I did not contract any Sexually Transmitted Diseases (STDs) or Sexually Transmitted Infections (STIs) during this encounter. I do know that God did not cause these things to happen, and I am grateful that he protected me through all the bad decisions not only by myself but of others. Life continued to throw me curveballs, and it quickly became apparent that my learning journey was far from over.

By the age of 19, I found myself a wife and a mother of two, homeless, relying on the goodwill of strangers for a place to rest me and my babies' heads each night.

Trapped in a cycle of seeking love, I soon realized that it wouldn't be forthcoming from my husband. My solution? Have more children. I started expanding our family, not simply for the joy one might find in parenthood, but as a means to quench my thirst for love. Eventually, I was faced with a decision to make for the sake of my children and myself. It didn't take long to realize just how self-absorbed my children's father—my first husband— was. There are many roles one can assume in life, and he made sure I filled them all. During our marriage, I was tasked with childcare, maintaining our home (when we had one), and managing the bills. I was a stone's throw away from being a single parent, but my deep-seated love for my children's well-being drove me to keep pushing forward, to never give up.

Eventually I decided it was time to end our marriage. I realized that even though I had a husband, I did not have a partner or companion. As the saying goes, "out of the frying pan and into the fire". Life continued to bear down on me, and it eventually became too much. At 25, I attempted to take my life. A life, mind you, I had yet to realize did not belong to me. Coming off a seven day fast from both food and water, I had what I thought was an epiphanic moment. I could make it all stop. The pain, grief, heartbreak, and struggling could all end. So, I took sleeping pills. I heard a voice telling me that if I laid down and went to sleep, I would never wake up again. Picturing my children's faces, I made my way to my sister-in-law's house. She forced me to vomit and helped to the best of her ability until the paramedics came. Once again, I heard a prompting in my spirit guiding me on what to say because I knew if I informed them that I attempted suicide they would take my children away from me. A fate far worse than death for me. After I eventually came to, I was told that I was resuscitated twice and was placed on life support.

With IVs in both arms, they tried to draw blood from my legs, but could not. I slept for three straight days. At that time, I heard two distinct voices, one said "come with me", and the other said "you can't have her, she's mine." The doctors could not believe what a miracle I was. They told me they knew I was someone special because another person would have lost their life within the first two days of being asleep.

That's when I experienced my "aha" moment. I finally understood that I was here for a purpose. I was on this earth to fulfill an assignment, and God would ensure His will was accomplished through each of us. At the age of 29, I joined the New Dimensions Church. There, I engaged in missionary work for five years. During this period, I also married my second husband. I genuinely believed he was a gift from God, an answered prayer. At the start of our union, he did nothing to contradict this belief. I thought, this is it! I can now have everything—a God-fearing husband who loves, hears, sees, and comprehends me.

Things were looking up for us. He landed a fantastic job with excellent pay and benefits, allowing me, for the first time, to not have to juggle all the responsibilities at once. Sadly, the new job also introduced a new man. He began to change. He grew distant, and it felt as though we were slowly becoming unequally yoked. I was finally able to breathe easy in life, so I chose to ignore the warning signs and focus on his positive attributes. Despite failing to build a connection with my children, he still provided for them. He would disappear for days on end, but when he was home, he devoted his time and attention to me. He became verbally and emotionally abusive, but I started blaming myself for this, as I couldn't provide him with what he desired most—a child. He managed the bills but neglected basic daily necessities like food or air conditioning in the summer. His straying from our marriage eventually led to infidelity. That was the final straw. I felt like a failure, watching my family crumble. My sons began to live life on the streets, and my daughter followed in my footsteps, becoming a young mother. Once again, I was confronted with a difficult decision. I chose to divorce my second husband.

Surprisingly, he concurred. He believed that I deserved better. He confessed that God had given him an angel and he hadn't known how to treat her properly. With these words, we parted ways. For four years, it was just me, the Lord, and my children.

For the first time since I had left home, I found myself alone. During those four years, plus eight months, I didn't belong to a church. Without any particular cause, I just ceased attending. Those four years also came with an unexpected surprise—I became a mother again. I wasn't sure I could handle it, considering my youngest child at the time was already 20 years old. All I could think was, "Lord help me, I have to start all over." When my youngest was eight months old, I began attending Triumphant in Christ International Ministries (TICIM), the church home of my now-husband. It was there that I started to understand what I had been missing in a partner and a true man of God.

As we were planning our wedding, my world was shattered once more. In 2013, my third eldest son, Quaddaro, was murdered. There I was, juggling the planning of a wedding and a funeral—it felt like the plot of a terrible movie, but it was my reality. I was overwhelmed with confusion and frustration. I questioned God. I was angry with Him. I couldn't understand why, just as my life was starting to fall into place, the rug was yanked out from under my feet.

On the day my son passed away, I went into his room while he was asleep. Something stirred in my spirit urgently. A voice said, "Look upon your son, because this is the last day you will see him alive." I didn't know whether to pray with him or stand outside the room where he was sleeping. I knew I wanted him to rest because he was tired that day, but the urgency in my spirit was too potent to disregard. I left the room and prayed. Still, I couldn't grasp the words I had just heard in my spirit. A part of me wanted to keep him at home to protect him, yet another part reminded me that he was an adult and I shouldn't be afraid because God hasn't given us a spirit of fear. I didn't realize then that it wasn't fear; it was a warning.

He later woke up and decided to leave. He gave all the kids money, hugs, and some of his personal items. We said our "I love you's" and he left. Now I wonder if he knew what was coming. Looking back, I remember how my son used to tell me about the nightmares he had concerning his own death. When you believe you have ample time, conversations like that become afterthoughts. "If I only knew then . . ." comes to mind now.

I remember scrolling through Facebook and seeing an "R.I.P" message with my son's name next to it. I thought, "No, this can't be right." I waited for him for two weeks, expecting him to walk through the front door any moment. I tirelessly called hospitals, morgues, and correctional facilities, unable to accept what I had seen on Facebook. Eventually, I reached out to the Ford Funeral Home, and Mrs. Ford offered to help me locate my son.

When she called the morgue and relayed the confirmation to me on a three-way call, the coroner informed me that my son was indeed there. However, I wasn't allowed to see him because his body hadn't been prepared yet. Unexpectedly, before I could view my son's body at the morgue, it was released without my permission to Edward's Funeral Home. In my frustration, grief, and despair, I contacted the Ford Funeral Home again, seeking their assistance in retrieving my son's body. Displaying understanding, compassion, and professionalism, they honored my request and coordinated the transfer from Edward's Funeral Home.

I had thought receiving the news of my son's passing was the most crushing part of this ordeal. But I was hit by another blow when I learned that his murderers had attended his funeral. My eldest son recognized them and informed me of this. At that moment, maintaining composure meant nothing. My pain, anguish, and raw anger erupted in incoherent screams. In my mind, I could only form the words, "Why, God, Why?" His answer came: "If not today, then tomorrow."

Despite my lingering anger with God, this response provided some comfort. I had to delve deeper, finding peace in the knowledge that Quaddaro knew God, and God knew him. He was now with his Father, his Creator, and would be well cared for.

This understanding offered me a much-needed source of strength.

I truly believe that my current husband is another manifestation of God's love for me. Amid the tempest in my life, we exchanged our vows. He stood by me during an extremely difficult and vulnerable time, loving me unconditionally. He demonstrated the qualities I had been seeking in a partner and a genuine man of God. He showed me how a man should love his woman and his children. Even after experiencing a tragedy in his own life—the loss of his first wife—he continued to love and tried to fill the void for his children.

In 2019, after leaving TICIM, I joined the Pursuit of God Church (POG) under the guidance of Apostle Ricky Floyd and Pastor Sheila Floyd. Although the Word of God was present at my former church, I felt that the calling on my life wasn't being nurtured there. As a member of POG, I began to sense more clearly that God was leading me towards prophecy and evangelism. I joined the intercessory prayer team, the evangelism team, and the children's ministry at POG. I wasn't entirely sure of their plans for the children's ministry, but I trusted God's guidance, even if He didn't reveal the entire plan to me.

At POG, there is a real sense of family. I feel at home and loved. I feel like I'm receiving everything I need from a place of worship. Under the leadership of Apostle Ricky Floyd and Pastor Sheila Floyd, I've managed to overcome many things that I had been clinging onto. They have been the parental figures that I have craved for my entire life. Thanks to Apostle Floyd's recommendation, I was blessed with the opportunity to share my son Quaddaro's story with the world through the documentary "Vanishing Kings".

Although my husband is not a member of POG, he enjoys contributing to their outreach ministry, the Husband Institute, where he can mentor young men. He is grateful for the chance to support the ministry because he believes in the good work they do. From the "projects" to homeownership, from not knowing love to experiencing it in many ways each day, from weathering storms to harnessing the power to calm the seas—my life has been a journey of transformation. I developed trust issues after my mother was murdered by the person she trusted most and thought was harmless, but I've learned to let go and let God guide me. From believing my father was dead to building a relationship with him in his later years, from lacking a positive male role model to marrying a man of God who mentors others lacking that figure—God has used my trials and tribulations to strengthen my trust in the foundation upon which my life is built.

Thanks to God, even though my two-year-old body was violated, it wasn't mutilated, and I could still have children. Thanks to God, despite enduring periods of such dire poverty that I stole to feed my children, I now have more than enough and can bless others. Thanks to God, despite living through long stretches of darkness, I can appreciate the dawn and recognize the many ways God loves and cherishes me. Many of the challenges I've faced have shaped me into a better person. They've taught me compassion for those enduring similar trials, wisdom and caution regarding who I allow into my life, and the importance of heeding the guidance of the Holy Spirit. We may not be able to see others' hearts, but God can.

I am thankful to God that through prayer and standing on His word, I've overcome what troubled me for much of my life. Now, I can genuinely rejoice and walk in the manifestation of that deliverance. I am thankful that all my children are thriving and, despite everything, the three great joys in my life—my God, my husband, and our children—have enabled me to stand against all odds.

"Even when you are homeless, been through some things, raising children on your own, only have a GED you can still stand on the Word of God and stand against all odds"

(Melba Gilmore-Cole, 05/2023)

Jacobs-Kayam A, Lev-Wiesel R. In Limbo: Time Perspective and Memory Deficit Among Female Survivors of Sexual Abuse. Front Psychol. 2019 Apr 24;10:912. doi: 10.3389/fpsyg.2019.00912. PMID: 31068879; PMCID: PMC6491862

Shinskey, J. (2021, Aug). This is Why We Can't Remember Our Early Childhood Memories. http://cnn.com/2021/08/13/health/childhood-memories-partner-wellness

LIFE BEGINS WHEN THE HEALING STARTS! DON'T COUNT ME OUT!

BOSS LADY DREY

Mardrey Wade Kiles, MS, LPC-MHSP is a dedicated therapist based in Tennessee, with special recognition as a trained EMDR Clinician. As a trauma-informed therapist, she proudly serves as the Clinical Director of The HEADShop, PLLC, a hybrid mental health practice founded in 2018.

Her academic journey began with earning a Bachelor of Science in Psychology, followed by a Master of Science in Professional Counseling, both from Victory University in Memphis, TN. She is currently pursuing a Doctorate in Behavioral Healthcare and Executive Clinical Leadership at Freed-Hardeman University, Henderson, TN.

At the heart of her work is a profound passion: addressing the mental and physical health disparities faced by Black Women and marginalized communities. She's deeply committed to challenging stigmas and dispelling the age-old myth of the "Strong Black Woman."

With over two decades of experience, Mardrey has dedicated 22 years to the mental and physical well-being of individuals. Her roles have varied from serving as the Administrative Office Manager for a prominent community healthcare center in Shelby County, TN, to the Shelby County Ryan White Case Manager and later as the Program and Quality Manager for the same program.

On a personal note, she is blessed with a supportive husband and two incredible adult children. They are also graced with two delightful grand Gigi babies. Life has bestowed so much to be grateful for, yet there remains a vast expanse of work ahead of Mardrey.

To offer a glimpse into Mardrey's philosophy, her favorite quote resonates deeply: "Our wounds are often the openings into the best and most beautiful parts of us."—David Richo

LIFE BEGINS WHEN THE HEALING STARTS! DON'T COUNT ME OUT!

Two things in life are more wicked than the devil: an evil and perverted man and a cold-hearted, mean-spirited female. Those two are likened to poison. You must be aware of both!

Sitting here, I try hard to remember what I was like. But with all my might and as hard as I try, I cannot see what that little girl was before "the act". The act changed my life and took over my childhood and my life until I was 40. I was never myself. I would never get that person back. "The act" that would take me on a long, arduous journey I thought I would never end. Yes, "the act". Some events remain cloudy for me. Some details are difficult for me to recall. I've been told, this can be a result of trauma so bear with me as I share my story.

I can't remember my age when I lay in bed being awakened to someone (a male) touching me and rubbing his "man part" on me. It was my uncle. I was confused and frightened. I was shocked, but I didn't say anything. Each time I stayed over at her house, I would be awakened the same way. It would happen again and again for as long as I can remember. I told him to leave me alone. I told him, "I'm going to tell on you," but he didn't care. That did not stop him. Now that I think about it, he was an evil-hearted and sick man. My aunt slept in the bedroom adjacent to the cart; two of us shared the cart in the hallway. She was less than 10 feet away. Her son slept about a foot from where I lay.

I remember my cousins and I discussing not wanting to go over there anymore because he was freaky. I said I was going to tell Grandma. And

I did. I marched myself in there to tell her. She was my favorite person in the whole world, and she was my world. My grandmother didn't want my mother to get upset. She knew my mother was tough. However, my mother suffered from a bleeding ulcer from the time she was 14. Back then, people thought bleeding ulcers developed from worrying too much, so she didn't want to worry Mama. She said she would take care of it, and I trusted her. It ("the act") didn't stop. He kept on doing things to me. Whenever I spent the night there, he would crawl his nasty tail into that bed and do things to me. He had gotten so comfortable that when she would leave us with him while she was at work, he would make me stay in the house while others played outside. Finally, I told Mama and my stepfather. They would have fought the Devil over me. It stopped, and I didn't have to spend the night there anymore. The trauma didn't stop there; I was scarred for life. It would seem that for years I had become someone else—someone full of rage. That cute baby girl was gone forever. I could never get her back or remember what she was like before "the act". I had become someone who just wanted to escape. I wanted to get away. As a little girl, I remember running as fast as I could, thinking that if I ran fast enough, I would take off. I would fly away!

My mama was so hurt after I told her what had happened. She felt betrayed, as she later told me. Mama trusted that I would be cared for while she worked overnight at the hospital. She paid my aunt to care for me. Mama was the best mom. She took good care of me, and we had fun together. I think I was about five or six years old when this happened. I can't quite remember my actual age. Working with clients, I've heard them say they can't remember how old they were or that their childhoods were like a blur. So was mine. The things I can remember, I wish I could forget.

The day I was violated, my life changed. It was a turning point for me. That was my turning point; the day he violated me. It was the day my mother's precious little mouse was no more.

From that day forward, I felt like I had a target on my forehead. When I stepped out of Mama's house into the world, I could never imagine people not seeing me the way my mother saw me. I did not know how to feel or think about my sexual urges as a child. These urges were a result of the trauma I had experienced. I knew it was something to be ashamed of, and I felt guilty. I didn't understand it. I knew I did not like girls, but playing house allowed us to act out what we could not forget.

Many other children must have experienced the same things as I have. There were so many who experimented with touch and sex after being inappropriately touched themselves. The CDC (2022) writes that 1 in 4 girls and 1 in 13 boys have been sexually abused in childhood, and 91% of perpetrators are identified as trusted family members or close friends1. That is a lot of destroyed souls. I found myself drawn to other damaged kids but did not connect with anyone. I avoided it because I always felt different. I walked around, hoping no one could see me. I wondered if they knew how dirty I was and if they could see the filthy things I learned.

At 14 or 15 years old, it was like sex on steroids. I can honestly say I did not like the thoughts that entered my mind or even the things I was doing. Some of them I wanted to erase, so I started getting high. I was never the type to follow anyone. I brought the weed to the cove which was a spot on the block near my house—this was the hangout—and shared it with my friends. I stole it from my stepfather's stash. By the time I was 15, I had begun getting high on weed and drinking liquor. This went on for years. I was high most weekends. I maintained above-average grades all through high school. I did just enough to get by. How much more could this mind take? Right!

When I started junior high school, some girls were fuming at me. They couldn't stand to see me coming. My presence sent them into a rage. I knew it too. I would go in a different direction most of the time to go home. However, I could not miss them when it was time to get on the school bus and go to school. Oh my God! Most of the time, I was terrified of them and the things they would say about me, like, "Look at her." "She thinks she's all that!" But, no . . . I didn't think I was all that. If only they knew. My self-esteem was five times lower than theirs on any given day, but they couldn't see it. They saw something in me that I couldn't even see in myself. This continued for about two years, until I got fed up with the bullying and harassment. I decided to take on these fools. I was going to take a couple of them out. So what did I do? I took a knife to school.

I waited for those ugly-acting, dirt-ugly witches to come into the bathroom. I had no idea that someone had gotten wind that I had a knife in my locker. Obviously, they weren't as tough as they portrayed themselves. They did not show up at the meeting place. Now, mind you. I went to the

---

[1] Centers for Disease Control and Prevention. (2022, April 6). *Fast facts: Preventing child sexual abuse |violence prevention|injury Center|CDC*. Centers for Disease Control and Prevention.
https://www.cdc.gov/violenceprevention/childsexualabuse/fastfact.html

guidance counselor almost daily to let her know these girls were bullying me and making my life unbearable. She tried to tell me this was girls' stuff, it would blow over, and we would all be friends one day. In other words, she was being dismissive of my complaints—fat chance; I did not want anything to do with these girls, ever. There was no way I wanted to be friends with such hateful, mean-spirited girls as these. However, when she found out I had taken a knife to school, I was the one who was suspended for 180 days while the bullies went scot-free without punishment or reprimand. They were free to bully someone else, as they did. They were angry little girls. Some had babies and were mamas by the 8th grade, but I was the one labeled the "bad girl," and I was furious. No one saw me! No one saw that I was the one hurting, angry, and bullied. Instead, I was left with a suspension on my record that would follow me for a long time.

This left me feeling that no one would see me or know who I was outside of what was on my record. So what did I do? I continued down the path of the "bad girl". I lived up to the "bad girl" persona, and when I did, I did it well. Most of the time, I just mind my own business, but what I set out to do as the bad girl resulted in self-destructive behavior. I smoked plenty of weed, sold even more, and drank plenty of Stag beer, Wild Irish Rose, and Silver Satin wine. I even had M/D tattooed on my thigh because Mad Dog 20/20 was one of my favorites.

Consensual sex. It made me feel in control. I controlled when I wanted to have it and who I wanted to have it with. Sex was the only thing that gave me a sense of power. This was my thinking at the time. When I got into the game, I was hard to handle. I almost forgot about when I was one of the founders of a gang. My cousins, who were visiting from Chicago, knew of all the Midwest gangs. They had some affiliations, taught us the tricks, which is how it all started. I don't want to mention names because young people are crazy now—nothing like when we were growing up. I only remembered this when I ran into an old friend. I kicked around a lot in the streets. Yes, that was us. And this is when I learned to kick asses and take names. It didn't stop the hating, but it stopped those haters. I was not out to bully anyone but I held my own. At least, that's how I saw it. It is a trip sometimes to hear the names of gangs in my city now and know where those names originated. These types of self-destructive behaviors had become habitual and also a result of the trauma I had experienced.

I was very well developed during my teen years. Before going to high school, I had big breasts, a tiny waist, and a nice butt. I couldn't make this up if I wrote fiction.

The women in the neighborhood took notice that I was well-endowed. They were mean and wanted to join in with their girls who were bullying me for the same reason. Or maybe it was the other way around. Could it have been that those girls were bullies because their moms were bullies? One day, my mom had to come outside to get one of the ladies off me because she thought I wanted her husband. I don't know what these women thought, but I did not want to be around those run-down older men. I wasn't even attracted to them. I was dumbfounded and could not understand where this hatred was coming from. As I said, I had a target on my forehead. But I was clueless as to why. This made for the most challenging time growing up.

Little did people know that I didn't like myself. I didn't know myself. I was walking around an empty shell. I remember my first real fight; this girl came to my house with a big group of people. She wanted me to come out so she could whip me; she used some choice words for me. And with my mom being as proper as she was, this was pointed out every time one of those haters was mad at me. My mom was floored; she couldn't believe they were bold enough to come to my house. She told them there was no way I would come outside and fight like an alley cat or something of that nature. My mom's boyfriend said, "Let her go." He was sick of these acts and said I needed to end this crap. He instructed me to go out there and whip her until she ran or asked for mercy. That I did. I beat her until I got tired, looked up at him, and he said, "She ain't tired yet." Then he said, "If anyone jumped in, they could get some too." He was tough. He came from Chicago. He didn't put up with any mess, either. Finally, the girl was tired of getting her butt beat, and afterwards, she would give me money for our weekend party stash in the alley—voluntarily, I must add. I never trusted her because she was inclined toward her female insecurities, and you never know where they would lead a person.

These experiences drew me deeper into myself. I always thought about what my purpose was for being alive. I never had suicidal thoughts or ideas in my teen years; I just found myself searching for my purpose. Those thoughts were inner; they were never out for discussion with my nonintellectual teenage friends at the time. I would go to the library during lunch breaks during school and check out books about religion. I was curious about God. I wanted to know things for myself. I never blamed God for what happened to me as a kid, and I wasn't mad at him either. Those thoughts never entered my mind, not at all. I did want to know why I was here in this world. In my subconscious, I knew there had to be a reason for my existence. I can't even say if I was subjected to pain or the feeling of pain.

However, I guess I did.

I recall that sometimes I would cut to relieve that deep inner disgust. In my therapy practice, clients exhibit self-injurious behaviors due to bullying, sexual abuse, and adverse experiences. These experiences would lead them to cut to relieve pain because of the disgust they felt toward themselves. I can relate to them, and I assume this is the reason I am such a great trauma therapist. Those feelings are all too familiar, and my insight is keen. Searching for my purpose would continue into my early to late 40s, taking me a long time to see where I belonged.

In my teenage years, I would have fierce fights with my mom, and sometimes they would be so bad that they would get physical. Did she not see that I was damaged? I was torn up. I was just messed up! What happened to me could not just be one of those things that happened. "Let's move on." I need some validation, some acknowledgement, from somebody. I needed somebody to ask if I was okay. I mean, to sincerely ask me how I felt about the violation and the pain that lingered with me. That violation caused so much grief in my life and so many shame-filled and guilt-ridden moments. If that had not happened to me, I would have been the model little girl I was before the trauma. Instead, my family called me wild, feisty, and out of control. So, I lugged around the grief of losing my innocence. I accepted the shame of my acts and the consequences. It was too much for a kid to bear. I don't think parents knew back in those times what to do. Mama was wrestling with her pain over what had happened to me. I realize that now. Her little girl had gone through something she never imagined would happen. I could never believe the world was such a dark and hideous place. I came from a privileged world of love and adornment. My mama adored me. My parents wanted me, and I knew that.

In the 12th grade of high school, I got pregnant. People in my family found out, and they beat my mother down. They told her I had no say in the matter. Her place in my life was to make me have an abortion. So, my mother asked me what I wanted to do. I told her I was keeping my baby. I finished my senior year of high school while five months pregnant. I was working at one of the major distributors of cosmetics in the country as a sales call representative, and I began this job at the beginning of my senior year. My boyfriend had as much trouble and trauma in life as I did, and he was coping by smoking crack, getting high, being young, and living free. My daughter was born, and it changed my whole life. I had to get a grip on myself. I had to protect my daughter from experiencing the trauma I experienced. I did not drink as much, and I had long stopped smoking marijuana and using any other illicit drugs. I still had not found my purpose. What I did find was my hustle.

I decided to go to school for dental assisting. I completed the course in 12 months. My first job was in a community health setting as a dental assistant. I enjoyed it, but the doctor quit, ending my position. I found a job in another community health setting and quickly became the office manager. I was 21 and felt I could take on the world. I bought my first house that year, and my daughter had her own room. We were not sharing a room anymore. We were living and surviving, but I was still not fulfilling my purpose. Something felt wrong, and I still could not ignore the crap women threw at me. Every job came with a bully or two. I don't know what these women saw in me. I could never figure it out. I left there. I went to a private practice office, worked there for a few years, and then moved on to insurance claims and customer service. I worked in insurance claims as a team leader and supervisor for about 13 years. I was prospering, and my life was different. I was still not living my purpose.

While working as an administrative office manager at the executive office of a large community healthcare organization, I realized I needed to go back to school.

We talked during my daughter's winter break from her first year of college, and she convinced me to go to school and check out what interested me. I went to a Christian liberal arts college and majored in psychology, and I finished in three years with a 3.59 GPA. I wanted to wait a year before I went back to pursue more college, but as fate would have it, the time was now. I received a call from the head of the psychology department. He asked if I was interested in starting school in the fall of the year, and they offered me a full scholarship. Well, of course, I couldn't turn it down. I started school in the fall of the same year that I graduated from the bachelor's program. I completed my master's degree in professional counseling three years later with a GPA of 3.73.

This, for the average person, would be a solid move, but remember, my thoughts were on a different plane. I was not operating at the level of an ordinary person. I did not know who I was, and I was not happy where I was. I felt like an imposter, and those paper degrees were stored in a box in the closet, meaning nothing to me. On to the next! What was the next venture for me? I could not answer that for myself, nor could anyone else.

The following year would prove to be a fight for my life. Why did I allow my aunt to move in with me? She had to leave her house for some reason, and I cannot recall why. People asked, "Why are you letting her stay with you?" I loved her. She was one of my favorites, and I never held any grudge against her for what happened to me as a child, and I felt she was as much of a victim as I was. My aunt moved in, and she turned my world upside down.

Before I let her stay, things were going well. I had gotten a home built, and we sold the old house. My daughter was in dental school, earning her medical degree in dentistry. Yes, that baby grew up and was fabulous. I'm so proud of her. She wasn't living at home anymore. At my house, it was just me and my son. I had a boyfriend I dated, and we were not living together. We had been dating for about 6 or 7 years. He would come over and spend the weekend sometimes. I was so in love with this man. I had never experienced that type of love with a man before. Besides my first love, my daughter's father, this guy was good to me, but he had some jealous tendencies. He didn't want to think about me with another man. My house guest picked up on this. At the time, I was a member of a Camaro car club. I was having the best time of my adult life. My son and I rode everywhere together. We were winning first place everywhere we went. People would come to us and be astounded at how mother and son are connected. We were winning car shows and having a blast.

On this one day, my graduation day, I had completed my master's program and planned to celebrate with family and my club at this hangout spot. I left home that morning to go to work, leaving my dude at the house to finish up some work for me. When I returned, everything seemed normal. I dressed, and we went to the graduation and the after-party. My dude was acting strangely, watching everyone and scowling at them. I asked him what was going on with him. He didn't say anything, but instead he broke a glass on the table with his hand. I was just floored and outdone. I could not believe his behavior. I had never seen this behavior in all the years we were dating. When we returned to my house, he was livid. He was forceful and wouldn't let me move throughout the house. I had to threaten him by saying I would call the police, so he left.

She left her room to try to speak with him, aiming to calm the situation. He looked at her, his expression clearly saying, "What the hell are you talking about?" Days later, he showed up at my doorstep. She warned me about him, suggesting I steer clear. Still, I ventured out and we talked. He apologized and promised no harm would come to me. I let him know I wasn't ready to face him, that I'd reach out when I was. He departed, but later texted, hinting at something amiss with her. He even suggested she didn't care about my son or me. I was taken aback.

The matter weighed on me. I sought counsel from my pastor, who, after hearing the details, urged me to distance myself from her for the sake of my peace. But while I was out with friends, disaster struck. My home was burglarized—a first in 14 years. My security system had alerted me, but I dismissed it, assuming she had triggered it. However, I returned to a shattered window, missing valuables to include jewelry and television, and a home in disarray. Shortly after, Aunt Kaye appeared, her demeanor defensive. Could she have been involved?

Time passed, and my dude reached out again. He shared insights he shouldn't have had. He claimed she had told him about lies I'd supposedly spread and even blamed my mother for ending my marriage. She informed him that my grandmother had gone to her grave with a lie I had made up about her. My mother always left me at her house to run in the streets and chase men—so far from the truth about Mama.

She was always sticking her nose in our business—another lie. I was so upset. All false accusations. Still, I did nothing. I still did not move on from that. I continued to let her stay. But then, a call at work from her daughter threw me off balance. Her words were jumbled, insinuating my mother's jealousy over our bond. As I managed my clients, she bombarded me with calls and texts – 68 in total that day. By evening, I'd reached my limit. I demanded my aunt and her clan leave my home for good.

When they arrived to collect their belongings, her daughter stormed in, damaging my wall. I attempted to mediate, but she pushed me. Overwhelmed, I retaliated. I lit into them like I was sending her back to hell. I beat her, old and new. I was so tired of her and my aunt. Their chaos had consumed me. I couldn't fathom the turmoil they reveled in. Together, they were a force of nature or I'd like to call them, some witches, stirring the pot wherever they went.

I felt all that old stuff seep back in—all my pain and torment. How dare my aunt try to tell my story, but her version of it? My mother was not a whore. I did not lie. It all came down on me like tons of bricks. I hated her! I thought she loved me! I trusted her! I felt she needed me. Only to find out she wanted to ruin my life! She was destroyed, so why not make my life a living hell like hers had been all those years? It brought back all those old feelings of self-hatred and hurt I had for myself. I felt dirty again. My family—I needed them to do something, but they went on like she hadn't done a thing to me. Some of them said I was crazy. I was the mean one. Some of them told me I needed to forgive her. What I needed was to heal. I needed to try to find a way to heal myself. My pastor even told me one day to ask her for forgiveness. Damn! It felt like I was walking in a dark tunnel. There was no sound. It was muffled, and I was stuck. I was stuck for years. My boyfriend, the love of my life, and I broke up. That was just one more drop in my bucket. I needed to take several weeks off from work. I was losing my mind. I had lost myself. How could I be worse than I was when I was molested or even bullied? Well, I was, and I was suffering. Everyone thought, even me, that it was because I broke up with my dude. Some of it was, but most of it was because I saw my life as vulnerable and fragile. I couldn't pray. My best friend abandoned me because, yes, I was challenging to deal with, but I also knew she was not even equipped to help me. Even more so, my mother asked me a question during this time. She asked me if she had made me weak, as if she were asking why I was so broken. My life broke me. No, she did not make me vulnerable. Things that had happened to me were finally coming down hard on me. It seemed the devil always tried to put his hands around my neck. If he could not destroy my mind as a child, he wanted to beat me with sex and drugs as a teen. That didn't work, so when I was 30, he tried to kill me with an aneurysm after childbirth. My life was a struggle—a real fight. Sometimes I wanted to fold, but I was usually ready to fight. I was so low. I couldn't even pray. I knew I knew God, and I knew the power of prayer. I have been down some roads where I didn't even know what to pray for or what to pray about. I didn't even feel like I could pray, and even in those times, I knew my faith in God had to be the vessel to carry me through.

One day I was at lunch when I ran into this friend whom I had not seen in over 20 years. It was Joy, and she brought words of joy with her. She asked me to step outside to talk. I was emaciated-looking, and I had lost 20 pounds. She told me about wonders that I knew came from God. How could she know these things? She told me I would be back with my boyfriend. We were going to be married. We would have a big house, and I would be blessed with finances. And we would help others heal and move forward with their lives as we had. She said there were prerequisites to the promise. I had to allow God to come in and heal my heart and my head. It took time. The healing did not happen overnight.

On another day, I ran into a girl about ten years older than me from my old neighborhood, and she told me things about myself as a little girl that I did not know. She told me I was the cutest little girl. I was the little girl the bigger girls on the block wanted for a little sister. I was so flattered. It was like searching for historical documents when searching for your genealogy. She told me things I did not know about myself. I did not see that darling little girl who was so loved. I often would think, "How could someone do what was done to me and not see me as my mother and family see me?" How did they not love me and want to protect me? Before my pain, I did feel loved. After it, I felt awkward, guilty, and ashamed—too much for a little girl to handle. It is a wonder that I am as sane as I am today. Whew! It's been rough!

I was so double-minded in my faith. I had all kinds of people talking to me about what to do. Some people thought it was ridiculous to think God would do those things that were spoken over my life. "God is not a microwave", they would say. He doesn't instantly do stuff like that. Well, I took him at his word. I could not attend the church I grew up in. She was a member. I'd heard stories about my mother and me that she had told people in church and in the neighborhood. Folks will believe the worst before they believe the good. I went to another church with a friend and got into the Word. My journey with God was different; I am sure it is for everyone. It was so special. I could see prayer working in another realm. I could pray, and then I saw answers to those prayers right before my eyes. God was working. It was not that he had to show me great things because he had carried me through before. He was healing my heart and mind. This process was so personal. I was building a spiritual life with God, not a religious one. I had to distinguish my spirituality from the religiosity I had subscribed to for most of my life. Church trauma is a real thing, just as adverse experiences are real. Being able to identify and name both was a relief and a release.

I am a peculiar person. I don't fit into any mold. Most people are intently trying to figure me out. Something that I found out with my maturity is that I am turned off when it comes to specific actions of others, like getting with groups and disliking someone or getting with others to mistreat someone. I know all too well how that feels, and that is one of the most common things to do. I am a genuine person. I am loyal to a fault. You must show me I can't trust you or have you in my space. God protects me. He also gave me a robust and keen sense of discernment. I often brawled with that side of me. In the past, I thought he was showing me something to act on. He gives me insight, so I will never be in the dark. It's protection. And the girls that didn't like me then still don't like me today, only now in the form of adult women. I know now they have insecurities. I am the seemingly "too sure" person in the room. The bottom line is that people are all too weird, and their motives do not align with yours.

I am a licensed clinical therapist who enjoys helping people navigate difficult life circumstances. I sit for 8–9 hours daily, assisting people in unraveling their traumas, hurts, and much pain. I pray daily for God to give me the tools to help his people through these things. I finally found my purpose. It feels beautiful. I have thorns on my side that are still there. I have had my Damascus Road and have come out with full sight. People have walked out of my life, thinking they were hurting me, only because they knew my heart and thought it would devastate me. But God. I know people's capacities cannot measure up to mine, and I am okay with that part. My family is healthy. I have blessed children and am living out my purpose. That is all that matters to me. This is my truth. God knows it better—what I cannot remember because of his protection and love, I won't fight to remember.

And this is my purpose too!

Acknowledgments

I thank my dear friend and Sis, Prophetess Marceline Williams. She is one of my best cheerleaders and encourages me to go for what I want. I would like to thank my mother, Shirley Stringer. She puts the "ump" in my triumph. My mother believes I can do anything! I would be stuck in my darkness without her nudges and pushes. She would not let me stay there. I love you, mom! Thank you for telling me every chance you get, "You are so pretty!" "You are so smart!" "You are special!" Without those praises, I would have drifted to a place of no return. This chapter is dedicated to my grandmother, Elizabeth Mitchell, my angel, and is a true testament to Proverbs 31:10-31.

I'M STILL STANDING

WANDA TAYLOR-WILSON

Wanda Taylor comes from a splintered family of neglect, abuse, and addictions. A native Memphian, she grew up in a single parent home with her mother. Her father battled a long-term drug addiction. She lived in two housing projects – Lemoyne Garden and Cleaborn Homes – and was raised around gangsters, pimps, drug dealers, prostitutes, drug addicts and alcoholics.

At the age of 11, Taylor became a substance abuser, experienced domestic violence at 13, became a teenage mother at 15, dropped out of high school at 17, was in and out of the jail at 18, and had an abortion by the time she turned 20. Taylor also has been homeless five times. She lived in The Salvation Army twice, two vacant apartments with her children, lived out of her mother's car, and slept on a church parking lot before. When Taylor turned 21, she decided to walk away from a lifestyle of corruption and accepted Jesus Christ as her Lord and personal Savior.

Taylor turned her life around for the better. At the age of 26, she returned to the classroom. At 28, she received her high school diploma from Messick Adult High School. Upon graduation, she attended Southwest Tennessee Community College, where she received a Technical Certificate in Substance Abuse Counseling and an Associate of Science degree in Human Service. Then she matriculated at the University of Phoenix and received a Bachelor of Science degree in Business Management. Taylor had finally arrived. She'd shaken off her old baggage and developed a new purpose and outlook on life. Next was the job market. An educator for 20-plus years, she worked for The Salvation Army, Serenity Recovery Center, Shelby County Rape Crisis Center, Department of Human Services, and Shelby County Child Support Office. In 2004, Taylor decided to go public with her life story and self-published the book "A Woman of God: An Inspirational Book for Women." People who read her life story were touched; and those she knew shared their own experiences. She was on to something special and began touching the lives of others.

In her spare time, Taylor has volunteered at various organizations to give hope to young teenage girls, women and men, who've traveled similar paths. Some of the organizations included St. Peter Home-Children, Shelby County Juvenile Court, Youth Village, CAAP, Inc., and the Mark H. Luttrell Correctional Center for Women. On August 5, 2013, Taylor founded Ladies In Need Can Survive, Inc. (LINCS), a nonprofit 501(c)(3) organization that helps troubled women to transition back into society. LINCS provides them with the opportunity to get their lives back on track – and many of them have done just that.

While volunteering is germane to reaching the "least of God's people," Taylor also reaches people as a motivational speaker and community activist. She's also a recipient of several honors and awards and has been featured on Trinity Broadcasting Network (TBN), heard on radio stations around the world, and featured in several magazines and newspapers. In 2021, Taylor received a resolution from Councilwoman Rhonda Logan and Councilwoman Michalyn Easter-Thomas. She also received a resolution and the key to Shelby County Government from Commissioner Willie F. Brooks Jr. and received a proclamation from Shelby County Mayor Lee Harris. She is a recent recipient of the 2022 Best In Memphis Award.

Over the last decade, God has opened so many doors for Taylor and her organization. For example, A few celebrities have befriended her and expressed an interest in her arduous work rebuilding the lives of troubled women, such as actor Cassie Davis (Bam from the Tyler Perry shows, plays and movies), who presented Taylor with an award on February 25, 2017; Dove/Stellar/Grammy Award winner Jonathan Nelson, who ministered at LINCS's 4th Annual

"Celebration of Life Benefit Concert" on October 8, 2017; Grammy Award winner Sheila Raye Charles (daughter of legendary Ray Charles), who ministered at LINC's 5th Annual "Taking My Life Back Conference" on October 6, 2018; actor Vivica Fox, who gave LINCS a financial contribution on Oct 28, 2018; Grammy Award winner Le'Andria Johnson, who ministered at LINCS's "Taking My Life Back Conference" on October 23, 2021 and "I Am Not My Past Women's Prayer Breakfast" on April 9, 2022; and Actor/Writer/Producer Anthony (aka Tony) Grant (from the Tyler Perry plays, movies, and shows), who performed at LINCS's 2022 "Black and Red Holiday Gala."

In December 2022, Taylor opened a boutique aptly named The Taylor Made Boutique, LLC. In January 2023, she was an extra in season 3, episode 12 of "Young Rock," a sitcom based on the life of professional wrestler and actor Dewayne Johnson (aka The Rock). In February 2023, she modeled for a major department store – Dillard's. And on June 17, 2023, Taylor will play a church lady in the hit stage play "The Pulpit Is Not A Playground " at The Cannon Center for the Performing Arts in Memphis.

Wanda Taylor is the mother of two successful daughters and the grandmother of five amazing grandchildren.

I AM STILL STANDING

I am still standing after all I've been through! No matter what happened in my past, no matter the dysfunction, abuse, lack, or struggle, I had to shift my thinking. I had to see myself differently. No more of the victim who never gets a break. As long as I think I'm a victim, it's going to limit my destiny. I won't trust God, I won't pray bold prayers, I won't believe for big dreams, and I won't expect God's favor.

> *"I focus on this one thing: Forgetting the past and looking forward to what lies ahead."*
>
> (Philippians 3:13, NLT)

Are you focused on forgetting the past? Many people do not fully understand what that means. Many people often wonder, "How can I forget something that's happened to me?" What this verse says is that you must choose to disregard your past so that it doesn't keep you from moving forward.

Becoming a woman of God was by choice and not by force. According to Deuteronomy 30:19, *"I call heaven and earth to record this day against you, that I have set before you life and death, blessings and cursing; therefore, choose life, that both thou and thy seed may live."*

In this passage of Scripture, God is giving us two choices: The first choice is the road of life, which leads to blessings. The second choice is the road of death, which leads to curses.

God loves us so much that He tells us to choose life – meaning you, me, our children, and our children's children can live an abundant life. No one is exempt from making this choice in life.

Before I gave my life to Jesus Christ, I was slowly dying in sin. I was on my way to hell. I was serving everything and everybody but God. I'd engaged in some of the sinful activities headed for destruction. Day after day, month after month, year after year.

I drank liquor, smoked cigarettes and marijuana, as well as primo. I went to the club three to four times a week. During this time, I gambled, partied, stole, wrote bad checks, sold marijuana and crack cocaine, fornicated, watched pornographic films, indulged in violence, and carried firearms. I admit I was a mess. I was wrapped up in a persona that was self-destructive and waiting to implode.

Eventually, I would abandon my children, abort a baby, get a tubal ligation (tubes tied), and was in and out of jail as a result of such a reckless lifestyle. I was unstable and could not see my way.

When I accepted Jesus Christ as my Lord and Savior, my way of living, thinking, and speaking had to change. The same for you. Your words have power. Use them wisely. God has given you and me the freedom to choose how we use them.

"The tongue has the power of life and death, and those who love it will eat its fruit."

(Proverbs 18:21, NIV)

As a believer, attending church, fasting, praying, and reading God's Word makes our Christian walk a lot easier. We must put aside our pride, sinful activities, bear the cross, and follow His Word. He tells us that when we try to preserve our own lives, in the end, we will lose it all. Satan is full of evil, deceptions, and lies.

Satan's plans are to kill, steal, and destroy us (John 10:10).

There isn't anything worth sacrificing our souls. Nothing. Zilch. Jesus said if we are ashamed of Him and the truth of His word, He will deny us before the Father and the holy angels. I had to pray long and hard and ask God to deliver me. He delivered me indeed from a sin-sick lifestyle, and I found out <u>accepting Jesus Christ is foundational, but living Holy is the key</u>.

After walking with God for a while and after my deliverance, I wanted a personal relationship with Him. I wanted to know His voice. I wanted to know what God felt like and how He felt about me. I wanted to tell Him all about how I felt and what I was going through. I needed to tell Him about my pains and my struggles. I longed to tell Him about my dislikes and desires. I wanted to share all my secrets with Him. I did. I wanted to feel His presence and amazing power. Most importantly, I wanted to be used by God.

"Before I formed you in the womb, I knew you" (Jeremiah 1:5)

God knew everything I was going to encounter in life – every step I took, every road I trod, every move I made. So, I thank God I am no longer blind to sin – for God created me for a purpose, and that purpose is His will for my life.

> *"For I know the plans I have for you," declares the Lord, "plans to prosper you and not to harm you, plans to give you hope and a future"*
>
> (Jeremiah 29:11).

This journey has not been easy. I have messed up along the way. I have disappointed God. I have made promises I did not keep. Sadly, at times I have allowed Satan to re-enter my mind with past thoughts. It's easy to get caught up if you take your eyes off God.

> *"Put on the full armor of God so that you will be able to stand firm against the schemes of the devil".*
>
> (Ephesians 6:11)

At one point in my life, I didn't know how to resist the devil. This scripture was key for me. Because you're a Christian does not mean the devil and his imps are going to let up. No, baby. They're not. We are forever on his hit list. Why? Because we will no longer live for the kingdom of darkness. Today, I choose to stand. God has brought me through too much to doubt Him. Allow me to share with you what I have been through and how God brought me out.

I Am Still Standing After Multiple Abusive Relationships

My life was tremendously impacted by my childhood. Growing up in a single parent household where I watched my mom as she was severely abused in relationships affected me in many ways. The choices I made were a reflection of the impact. I began looking for love in all the wrong places and found myself involved in toxic relationships. At the age of 11, I was introduced to sex and other sexual related activities.

At fifteen, I got involved with an older guy. This relationship led to physical, mental, and verbal abuse. I stayed in the relationship for three years and suffered greatly while in it. He was my first love and I declared I would never open my heart to another man.

Forgiveness was one of the greatest challenges in my life. Why? I buried my pain, silent frustrations, and hate on the inside of me. There wasn't structure, values, or balance in my life growing up. Research shows that a father's influence in his daughter's life shapes her self-esteem, self-image, confidence, and opinion of men. It can even affect her love life and ability to trust. Growing up without a father figure was tough. I agree 100% with the researchers. You will understand why as you continue to read my story.

All my relationships were based on lies, deceit, cheating, and using men for money. I experienced one bad relationship after another. When I turned 18, I moved into my first apartment at Lemoyne Garden. Yes, it was considered the "projects." Shortly after living there I started selling marijuana. I liked having money and getting it quickly. For this reason, I dropped out of school in the 12th grade.

One day I was walking down the street and met an older guy who took interest in me. We started dating and as time went on, he started abusing me physically, mentally, and verbally. One night, he was so angry with me because he thought I had cheated on him while he was in jail. He continued to ask as if he wanted me to tell him I'd cheated. He even questioned if the baby I was carrying was his. I had not cheated and the child I was carrying was his.

One day, I was fed up, and I told him it's best for us to separate from each other. I packed everything that belonged to him and went to my neighbor's house to call him a cab. I knew he was going to beat me if the cab didn't come soon. We were sitting on the couch, and he was getting high. I kept repeating to myself, "Cab, please come. Please come, cab."

The drugs kicked in and anger took over. He made me take off all my clothes and tied me up completely. I was crying and mumbling because my mouth was tied up. I was pleading with my tears so he wouldn't kill me.

He explained to me that no one saw him come into the house. "I am going to burn you alive," he told me. Then he took a knife and placed it to my belly. He said to me, "I am going to cut your baby out of you." I was scared and helpless! I didn't know Jesus Christ, but He knew me. God did not allow him to kill me and my baby. Hallelujah!

It didn't stop there. The next day, he started questioning my best friend about me cheating on him. He was threatening to kill her too if she didn't tell the truth. She told him what I did. He then took a plank and beat me with it. I fell and he started stomping me. She was watching as he was abusing me. I said to him, "You're going to kill me and my baby if you don't stop." God spared our life again.

Hallelujah!

The day after that, he came to my job and made me leave work. He took me back to the same backyard and beat me with a rope in a shed. He was so angry because I had cheated on him. Shortly after that, he went back to prison, and I gave birth to our daughter. She looks just like him.

God brought me through these situations and others to let you know He is able to heal, deliver, and set me free in Jesus Christ's name. Keep in mind I was not saved and did not know the Lord, but He spared my life anyway.

When I gave my life to the Lord, I forgave my child's father and asked him to forgive me. I told him about generational curses and how Satan comes to destroy families. I shared with him that God would save, deliver, and set him free if he would repent, ask Jesus Christ into his heart, and allow God to show him the way. God would wipe his past away and give him a brand-new life.

I was in another sinful relationship with a guy. I got pregnant with my third child. He told me he did not want our child and paid for the abortion. From that day forward, I was not the same. As a continuous result of sins, entrapment began. I watched my mother and other members of my family date married men and women. I decided to date married men too.

"I dated a married man that lasted approximately one year. His reason for cheating on his wife was that she had a hysterectomy, and her body did not please him any longer. I used him for his money, and he used me for my body.

I also dated another married man that I worked with. Keep in mind that I was still not saved at this point. Almost every man I dated was older than me. This guy was not happy with his wife either. That was the lie he told me. Many times, he told me he was going to divorce her so we could be together. Did he divorce his wife? No!

He was my candy man, and I was his "play thang." At that point in my life, the only things that mattered to me were married men, money, drugs, and partying. I was a foolish young woman (I gave my life to God when I was 21 years old.) I recently gave my life to God, and the devil still had his hooks in me.

When I wanted him to stay home with me, I would call his job and tell his boss that he was sick and not coming in. I even drove his wife's car and his car when needed. I knew where he lived and called his house. I used to cash his checks. Last, but not least, I had his permission to check on his wife's personal business. Talking about boldness.

While on a date with a single guy, I received a text from the married guy saying, 'I have a package for you.' I made an excuse to end the date with the other guy, and I went to his house to see what he had. We sat down and talked about what was happening in his marriage. The next thing you know, I was in his wife's bed making love to him."

He told me she no longer lived there. I believed him and spent the night. God woke me up early that morning so I could leave but I did not obey His voice. I laid there half-naked while he was completely naked on the couch. God allowed him to hear the door as his wife turned the doorknob. He jumped off the couch and slammed the door in her face. She was crying and pleading with him and begging him to let her in the house. He told his wife that she could not come in.

From where I was, I could hear her say, "I am going to bust all the windows out of this "bit—h's" car and flatten her tires."

He replied, "If you touch that car, I will kill you."

I was thankful that God did not allow her to bust my windows out or flatten my tires. She did, however, pick up some bricks and busted three of the windows out of their home. While still in the house, I called the police and explained to them what was happening. Then I called my church, and I asked my First Lady Kendrick to let me speak to Quita. First Lady Kendrick told Quita that it sounded like I was in trouble. I told Quita about the situation I was in. One thing I've learned about a Pastor or First Lady is they can tell when something is wrong with a church member.

At this point, I didn't know what to do, I needed somewhere to hide. Every place I looked in the house, all I saw was her and their children's things. I said to myself, "This negro lied to me." I was upset because he lied to me about her moving out.

The police arrived at the house. The husband talked to the police through the door. The police asked him why he wouldn't let his wife come into the house. He told the police she's crazy and he doesn't want her anymore. The police asked him if she lived here, and he said yes.

God was ministering to me in the midst of sin. God told me to go out the front door and stand behind the tree. I stood on the porch saying to myself, "I want her to see me." God told me a second time to go stand behind the tree. I did not obey his voice. God said it a third time, with bass in his voice, "Go stand behind the tree." I was so upset, but I chose to obey God's voice the third time He spoke.

He finally let his wife in the house, and they started arguing. The police were walking to their cars and noticed me.

"Were you in that house?" they asked. "Yes, I was in the house," I answered. They asked me if I knew he was married. I answered, "No."

"If that woman had caught you in her house, she would have killed you," the officer explained.

The officer said, "every other day we are at their house because they're always trying to kill each other." The officer asked how I was going to get my car out of their driveway. His wife had parked her car close to my bumper. So, I was told to drive across the neighbor's grass and never come back to the house.

I left their house and went straight to church. I was asking the Lord to please forgive me and deliver me from this relationship. But I did not stop. I felt this married man owed me. I kept calling him and spending his money. God showed me in a dream that if I didn't stop, I was going to die. From that day forward, I never got involved with him again. I thank God for sparing my life. Despite my sins, God gave me a way of escape. So, ladies, if you are in a situation like this, please ask the Lord in the name of Jesus Christ to deliver you.

August 20, 2022, I married my best friend, my soulmate, my partner, and the love of my life, Mr. Derrick Wilson.

I Am Still Standing After Long-term Drug Addiction

I was dating this guy who was not healthy for me. One day, he and his brother came over to my apartment. I was cleaning up and his brother was sitting at my table rolling up. I asked him to roll me a joint. He did what I asked and without my knowledge he had laced it with something. I sat down on the couch and I took a hit, and then another hit. My youngest daughter crawled over to me, and I picked her up. My arms grew weak and dropped my daughter on the floor. My oldest daughter noticed something was wrong with me. She said, "Mommy, what's wrong." I was drifting off.

Then she spoke again, "Mommy, you can't fall asleep. Wake up, Mommy, wake up." When I came to, I asked her to pass me the phone quickly. I contacted my cousin Duke and told her I felt like I was dying, to call the paramedic, and my Mommy. "Please!" Thank God my daughter was able to keep me awake until the paramedics arrived. I was rushed to the emergency room and whatever the drugs were laced with, the doctor flushed it out of my system in time.

When a person is under influence they do not think clearly or make the right decisions. This was me. I will never forget this one particular day, I was giving my daughter a bath and shampooing her hair. She screamed and hollered, and my nerves couldn't handle it. So, I began to scream, "Shut up, shut up! I am not going to tell you again to shut up."

I heard a loud voice say, "hold her head under the water and she will stop crying". Then I heard another voice. It was soft, calm and it said, "Wanda, no"! Snapping out of it I screamed, "Noooooooo!" I grabbed my baby out of the tub and held her tightly to my heart. Keep in mind I was not saved.

You will not believe the child the devil wanted me to kill was that same child who saved my life when I took my last hit. If it weren't for my oldest daughter, Kenisha, I could have died or worse. I could have suffered from a mental illness.

Kenisha is a remarkable woman. She is a mother of four, a devoted wife, a three-time college graduate, a retired sergeant from the United States Army, and now just one year away from becoming a doctor. Throughout her journey, the devil tried to hinder her progress, but his attempts were in vain. Her life is a testament to how the enemy will try to kill you and your destiny but God has the final say so.

My youngest daughter is equally inspiring. As a mother of one child, she has embraced the joys and responsibilities of motherhood. She is a loving wife and a successful entrepreneur, showcasing her dedication to both family and professional pursuits. I thank God for my daughters and the women they have become.

All glory to God, December 31, 2023, will mark 28 years clean and sober from drugs.

I Am Still Standing After Being Arrested Numerous Times

I moved to the "hood". It didn't take long before I was caught up again. I started selling marijuana to the "dope boys" in the hood. I met this guy, who later became my boyfriend and baby's daddy. He taught me how to push crack cocaine. I wanted to look like a drug dealer, so I went to the dentist to have five gold teeth fitted in my mouth. I played the part and looked like the part of a despicable drug dealer, not realizing that I was drifting into an immoral lifestyle.

I was caught up. That immoral lifestyle caused me to hurt myself, my children, and other people. I was killing the people in my community by selling them drugs. I was ruthless. I would kick in doors and pull guns on people who owed me money. I was fearless. I would go after my money in broad daylight. This was my life at least, until this lifestyle landed me in jail. I was convicted which resulted in an eviction from my apartment. I spent almost all of my money on bonding out of jail, paying lawyer fees, probation fees, court costs and fines. I became homeless again for the second time.

I was tired and ready to give up the street life. I just wanted a new beginning. A few months later, we moved into our own apartment again. Guess what? I started selling drugs all over again. I couldn't break this vicious cycle. The devil had his hooks in me. It was obvious that I did not learn my lesson the first time. I started 'running' the streets again until one day, I realized that if I didn't change my ways, it would lead to a tragic end—either death or a long jail sentence. Feeling desperate, I turned to God, asking for deliverance from the dangerous path I was on. Miraculously, my prayers were answered when I made a firm decision to change. I found myself crossing paths with the people I had hurt in the past, and with tears in my eyes, I sincerely apologized and asked for their forgiveness. It was amazing to witness the power of God's presence, as tears of emotion streamed down the faces of those I had hurt. I tried to offer encouragement, minister to their needs, and show them love. The moment I heard the heartfelt words, "I accept your apology and I forgive you, Wanda," it deeply touched me. That's when God's reality became apparent in my life, and I realized that He could help me right my wrongs.

I Am Still Standing With Purpose

I had dropped out of school in the 12th grade, and it was time for me to turn my life around for the better. At the age of 26, I decided to return to the classroom and pursue my GED. However, despite my desperate efforts, I couldn't pass the test after three consecutive attempts. Frustration and a sense of failure weighed heavily on me, especially when the test changed to a HiSET curriculum.

One morning, while I was heading to Messick to discuss my options with the administrative staff, a young woman stopped me, recognizing me as the lady who prayed for others during the GED tests. She shared that some people had passed their tests, and that encounter sparked a realization for me. God reminded me that my journey back to school wasn't solely about myself, but rather to encourage and pray for others.

At the administrative office, I was asked about my previous education, and I disclosed that I dropped out in the 12th grade but believed I had passed the TCAP test. Through further inquiry, we discovered that I only needed 5 ½ credits to obtain my high school diploma. This revelation filled me with hope, and I promptly enrolled in the adult classes at Messick Adult High School.

Balancing school and raising two children wasn't easy, but with the help of my aunt, Moma Prune, who owned a daycare center, I managed to attend classes day and night for ten and a half months. On October 15, 2002, I proudly walked across the stage and received my high school diploma at the age of 28.

Graduation marked a turning point in my life. I went on to Southwest Tennessee Community College, where I earned a Technical Certificate in Substance Abuse Counseling and an Associate of Science degree in Human Service. Later, I continued my education at the University of Phoenix, obtaining a Bachelor of Science degree in Business Management.

My journey didn't end there. In November 2002, I began hair school at Tennessee Technology in Memphis while working part-time. The road was tough, especially when an accident involving a bus driver driving under the influence led to the termination of employees with past drug charges. I had to face the Department of Human Services Child and Adult Day Care Licensing Department to resolve my case, but with unwavering faith, I emerged victorious.

After overcoming various challenges, I completed cosmetology school on February 26, 2004, thanks to the support of those around me and the financial aid I received. I proudly received my Cosmetologist diploma on February 28, 2004.

In 2004, I shared my life story with the world through self-publishing a book titled "A Woman Of God – An Inspirational Book For Women." And on August 5, 2013, I took another significant step by establishing "Ladies In Need Can Survive, Inc.," a transitional home offering a second chance to women in need. My journey has been filled with struggles and victories, but through faith and determination, I've arrived at a place of fulfillment and purpose.

I Am Still Standing

As a motivational speaker and community activist, my journey has been marked by numerous honors and awards, and I have been recognized on various prestigious platforms. I've had the privilege of being featured on Trinity Broadcasting Network (TBN), reaching audiences on radio stations worldwide, and being spotlighted in several magazines and newspapers.

Over the past decade, the grace of God has opened countless doors for me and my organization, allowing us to make a significant impact. Notably, I've had the opportunity to build meaningful connections with some notable figures, including actor Cassie Davis, known for her role as Bam in Tyler Perry's shows, plays, and movies; Dove/Stellar/Grammy Award winner Jonathan Nelson; Grammy Award winner Sheila Raye Charles, daughter of the legendary Ray Charles; Actress Vivica Fox; Grammy Award winner Le'Andria Johnson; Actor/Writer/Producer Anthony (aka Tony) Grant from the Tyler Perry plays, movies, and shows, and No. 1 Billboard Gospel Artist JOKIA.

In December 2022, I achieved another milestone by opening The Taylormade Boutique, LLC, a boutique that aligns perfectly with my vision. Following that, in January 2023, I had the privilege of being an extra in season 3, episode 12 of "Young Rock," a sitcom based on the life of the renowned professional wrestler and actor, Dwayne Johnson (aka The Rock). The following month, I had the incredible opportunity to model for a major department store—Dillard's.

Additionally, I was proudly featured in a major stage play titled "The Pulpit Is Not A Playground" at The Cannon Center for the Performing

Arts in Memphis. Throughout my journey, I have managed to earn three college degrees, a testament to my determination and perseverance. As I reflect on my life's journey, I find inspiration and strength in Jeremiah 29:11, trusting that God's plan for me has been fulfilled, and I firmly believe that if He did it for me, He can certainly do it for anyone else too.

My story is a testament to the power of faith, resilience, and the willingness to pursue one's dreams despite challenges. Through my work and experiences, I aspire to motivate and uplift others, showing them that they too can overcome obstacles and achieve their goals with unwavering faith in God's guiding hand.

NOW I'M STRONGER

DEORA CLAIRÉ

Blessed with a resonant mezzo-soprano voice, Deora Clairé is a Christian bilingual singer-songwriter hailing from the musical heartland of Memphis, TN.

Raised in the inner city, her parents emphasized the vital roles of faith and education in life. Deora attended church every Sunday, singing hymns with fervor, and was a diligent honors student throughout the week. She was actively involved in several choirs and a variety of other extracurricular activities. Her enthusiasm for learning also extended to the Spanish language. She further cultivated this passion during her college years, which included a study abroad stint in Costa Rica. In 2016, Deora earned a Bachelor's degree in Spanish, complemented by a minor in International Business.

In 2018, while balancing her full-time role as a Bilingual Marketing Specialist, Deora released her first body of work, an EP titled Love Over Hate. Although comprising only three songs, this release bolstered her confidence in her creative abilities. Consequently, in the summer of 2019, she released three remixes of her original song "Forget You," filmed her first music video, and gave her inaugural performance at the Delta Fair.

However, the summer of 2019 also brought personal challenges that impacted Deora's mental health, causing a pause in her musical journey. After a period of self-reflection, she released her debut album, Golden, in January 2022. The album is a musical chronicle of her hiatus. August 2022 saw the release of her second album, My Life, featuring the song "Destined for Victory". This empowerment anthem expresses renewed self-confidence and identity in God, while the album's other Christian-themed songs aim to aid others on their faith journey.

Additionally, Deora Clairé is an author. She wrote a devotional called "Taking Action Against Depression", which was launched in March 2023 and can be found on the Bible App by YouVersion. In the devotional, she provides guidance on overcoming depression.

Currently, Deora is engrossed in the creation of new songs, an upcoming album, more devotionals, and a book. She is thrilled about God's plan for her life and eagerly anticipates the opportunity to positively impact the world for His Kingdom.

NOW I'M STRONGER

Before I experienced the worst part of my life, I was on cloud nine. I considered myself to be a young lady of 23—beautiful, smart, bilingual, and having earned my bachelor's degree in three years instead of four. I had just left working at one of the top nonprofits in the nation to pursue my dreams of being a singer-songwriter. I believed my next move was my best, but little did I know that the worst was lurking around the corner.

It all started in July of 2019 with my first manic episode, which is a characteristic of bipolar disorder. During this episode, I experienced high energy, delusions, and disorganized thoughts as well as emotional stress from a breakup I initiated due to infidelity on my ex's part that triggered me, and I wasn't handling it well. I recall wanting to go to the spa and relax since I had trouble sleeping for a few days.

On the day I planned to go to the spa, I got locked out of the house. Therefore, I decided to lay in the middle of our neighborhood's cove on a blanket so I could look at the clouds on that beautiful July day. I honestly thought it was a great idea until I saw my parent's car coming and had to move out of the way. They asked me what I was doing, and I told them I wanted to look at the sky since I got locked out of the house. I then began to walk to the vacant houses in the cove and speak to them because I thought I could hear and feel their spirits. My unusual behavior prompted them to call for help.

Before I knew it, instead of going to the spa, I was taken to the hospital and was led into a private waiting room with my parents. I was livid because I really wanted to go to the spa. I started walking around the private waiting room yelling. I was so delusional that I thought there were lions in the three closets of the waiting room, and I was commanding them to come out. When they did not come out, I yelled even louder. I was upset about everything: the breakup and not going to the spa.

When it was my turn to be seen, the psychiatrist committed me. They transferred me to a mental hospital without my knowledge, and I was not happy with whatever was going on, so I screamed loudly to the point where they had to give me something to calm down.

Upon my arrival at the hospital, they had me strip down naked and change into some thin hospital scrubs, which I had helped to do since I was out of it. I had no bra and no panties underneath. I didn't know where I was and everything felt surreal. I was walking along the halls and was trying to figure it out when I saw what seemed to be a "friendly" man open his arms for a hug. I went to him for a hug, and then the unspeakable happened.

While hugging me, he slipped his hands in my pants' (scrubs) and put a finger inside me. He fingered me for a couple of seconds and then tasted his fingers. He said something, but I was so dazed at everything that happened, I don't recall his words. Next thing I remember is someone hurriedly pulling me away. I was frozen and didn't know what to do. It didn't register that I had been violated until a day or so later in my stay at the hospital.

Half the time I was there, I was trying to figure out where I was, how I got there, and what I was supposed to do. I followed orders: took the medicine, went to group therapy, and participated in healthy coping skills like coloring and reading the Bible daily—it was my true source of comfort. When I saw the man again, he sat down beside me and extended his hand for a handshake. He didn't say anything. I paused, looked at his hand, and shook it. I couldn't look up. It would have been too painful, and I didn't know what else to do.

When I look back on it, I think he was trying to be forgiven for what he did. I do forgive him now but the empty feeling inside at that moment was still very present. For days I didn't eat much at the hospital—only enough to survive. I was traumatized from the experience overall. It was too much: the break up, the mental hospital, the molestation. Even when they released me after being there for seven days, I still didn't feel like myself.

It turned out that I was experiencing depression for the first time in my life. My days were lonely and filled with tears. Despite that, I forced myself to go out with my best friend to celebrate my "golden birthday." I turned 24 on the 24th of July, but I didn't feel anything close to golden. I also believed that I couldn't continue pursuing my dreams of being a singer-songwriter with a mental illness, especially considering my current mental state. I felt utterly broken and couldn't fathom why God would allow such experiences to happen to me. Nonetheless, I held onto my faith.

Since my first day in the mental hospital, I made it a point to read the Bible every day. As a preacher's kid, I was well aware that even in the midst of my struggles, God was still by my side. I prayed constantly, whether on my knees or sprawled out, pouring out my heart to Him because I trusted that He was the only one who could provide assistance . . . and He did.

Within two months, I managed to secure a new job and put on a brave face every day. I chose not to share with anyone what I had been through. I couldn't believe that I had been diagnosed with bipolar disorder, nor did I want to accept that I had been molested. I was pretending to be the old me—the smart, confident, and beautiful version of myself—while secretly mourning the loss of the old Deora Clairé. Eight months of this charade passed before I attempted to set things right in March 2020.

I was on a date with a male friend at his place, and I was thinking if he fingered me then that would erase the molestation. I totally believed the delusion though I didn't tell him my thought process. He fingered me as things were heating up, and I still felt the emptiness. Hours later after I left his place, I was in a full blown manic episode. After this, and unbeknownst to me, I was driving around Memphis thinking I was invisible and ended up walking around an apartment complex butt naked. By the grace of God, some nurses saw me and covered me. Then a cop arrived and one of the nurses went to talk to them. They gave me the option to either go to jail or go to a mental hospital. Even in the terrible mental state I was in, I decided to go to a mental hospital, but I begged them to not take me to the one I went to at first because I was scared the violation was going to happen again. Therefore, they drove me to a different mental hospital, and I was committed for 10 days. During my stay, I actually enjoyed the treatment I received. I took medicine, went to the gym, participated in group therapy, played games and received visits from my family until COVID lockdown began.

When I was released, my job was remote and I began working from home. Thankfully, my workload was light to where I barely did anything which was perfect because my days at this point involved me taking medicine daily for bipolar disorder while going through the toughest depression ever. I battled suicidal thoughts constantly. I didn't want to live, and I didn't feel worthy to live. I was numb and not acting like myself at all. I would pray, but it didn't feel like life was getting any better. But then God reminded me of Jeremiah 29:11, "For I know the plans I have for you," declares the Lord, "plans to prosper you and not to harm you, plans to give you hope and a future." This verse changed my life. I clung to it because my life depended on it. Inspired by this scripture, I began to write my first song since the diagnosis. I titled it "Purpose." In it I reminded myself that I was born with a purpose. I'm chosen anointed, and that no matter what comes my way I wear a crown. I'm distinguished and worth it because within me is God's spirit and power! I sang this song every day. With God, medicine, and therapy, I got through the depression.

I learned that God will send you the right people at the right time to help you on your journey, and my mental health team made up of my psychiatrist and therapist were two of them. They were the first people I told about the molestation about a year after it happened. I think the reason why I didn't want to talk about it is because that would mean I had to admit it happened to me, but opening up brought relief and comfort. When I told my parents, they were sad and upset. My father suggested I take legal action. I didn't choose to do so because I felt like it wouldn't do anything. It wouldn't change the fact that I was molested. Plus, I understood that the person who violated me was also in the mental hospital being treated for whatever mental issues he had and therefore, preventing the case from being held together because he was mentally incapacitated. I felt like I would lose after I've already lost so much.

Moving forward, I continued to pray and read the Bible daily. It helped me heal and truly forgive. God also reminded me of Romans 8:28, "And we know that for those who love God all things work together for good, for those who are called according to his purpose." I had faith that God would use the breakup, bipolar disorder (manic/depression episodes), and molestation for my good. I understand it's hard to believe that and it sounds so wrong. Like how can God turn these negatives into positives? Well let me tell you.

Sharing my testimony of what I've been through so far, has brought healing to the places where I was wounded. Because of my shares, I have received love and support instead of shame and judgment. Furthermore, I've understood the reason why I can't give up on myself, my dreams, and my life. It's because God has a purpose for me that has to come to fruition which requires my participation. My purpose is to encourage and expand God's Kingdom by spreading messages of faith, hope, and love through my testimony, songs, devotionals, and books. My life will be an example that God can use everything, good and bad in our lives, to bring His purpose for us to pass.

Lastly, I believe God used the breakup, bipolar disorder, and molestation to strengthen my relationship with Him and to help those who have been heartbroken, dealt with mental health challenges, or even violation. I want to encourage you with this, "No matter what you have gone through or will go through, God will use it to make you stronger, wiser, and better than you were before. With God, you are more than a conqueror (Romans 8:37). With God, all things are possible (Matthew 19:26). With God, you can have life abundantly (John 10:10)."

Acknowledgements

First, I would like to thank and give praise to God for this opportunity to share my story. I am grateful for Mrs. Marceline Williams, TJ Woodard, and all of the strong ladies I share this book with.

To my family and friends, I love and appreciate all of your support through the challenges I've experienced. Because of your encouragement, I have the courage to tell my testimony.

Contact Info
www.deoraclaire.com
info@deoraclaire.com

THE FINAL ESCAPE

RANISE MICHELLE JACOBS

Ranise Michelle Jacobs aka "Gracie Michelle" meaning (Blessed with a Gift from God), is the author and publisher of Women Exhaling and Excelling Journal. She's also the author and publisher of EnVision Inspiration Magazine. Ranise is a Wellness Consultant, she enjoys the art of talk therapy. She also enjoys the art of writing inspirational poetry and motivational articles that will help motivate women to improve their mental health, process grief and loss, manage stress and anxiety, and to accomplish their dreams and goals. Ranise does her best writing in front of the window, with open blinds, which she creates as a peaceful, calm, and relaxed serene Zen Den writing space. In addition, Ranise is a professional photographer, in which she does business under EnVision Photography and Publications. She specializes in natural outdoor oasis and special event photography.

Ranise is a pre-licensed Family Therapist, pursuing clinical hours for licensure to become a License Family Therapist. Ranise currently holds a Master of Science in Marriage and Family Therapy; Capella University,

Bachelor of Science in Business Management; University of Phoenix, Bachelor of Theology in Religious Studies and Christian Counseling; Jacksonville Theological Seminary and Bible College, and an Associate of Science in Liberal Studies and Substance Abuse Counseling; Southwest Tennessee Community College.

Ranise is passionate about helping women and their children, to overcome life challenges and crisis situations, such as; relationship issues, youth and young adult issues, divorce, grief and loss, traumatic events, substance abuse, mild depression, generalized anxiety, panic, social anxiety, and phobia disorders. Also, breast cancer crisis. She specializes in "Relaxation, Stress and Anxiety Management Therapy, and Emotion Regulation Therapy". Ranise is currently employed with the Shelby County Sheriff's Office Jail Division, where she has over 30 years of employment in the Corrections Field. She holds the position as a Programs Supervisor in the Programs Department. She is experienced in helping residents prepare for reentry back into society and the workforce, by providing residents with behavioral modification group sessions to include Anger Management, Substance Abuse, Restorative Arts, Thinking for A Change, and Employment Readiness programs during their detainment. Ranise specializes in helping residents transition from jail to community Substance Abuse and Job Placement programs.

Ranise enjoys the Visual Arts of; photography, graphic design, inspirational and motivational writing, acting, and decorative design. She also enjoys traveling, thrift shopping, socializing with family and friends, and spending quality time with her adult children and grandchildren. Ranise is a three-year Breast Cancer survivor and is also passionate about talking to women regarding the importance of getting their annual mammograms, maintaining a positive self-concept, and feeling beautiful about their self-image when experiencing the breast cancer journey.

Gracie Michelle

Emails: ranisejacobs@gmail.com
envisioninternational2015@gmail.com Websites:
https://www.envisiontheoccasion.com
https://www.womenexhalingandexcelling.com

THE FINAL ESCAPE

An Overcomer is defined by your **FAITH**. Your **FAITH** is defined by your ability to **BELIEVE** in **GOD**, to give you the **STRENGTH** and the **COURAGE**, to help you survive an _emotionally_, _physically_, and _financially_ controlling relationship. "I was afraid, and the thought of leaving filled me with fear, but I knew I had to depart to preserve my sanity. I felt as though I was in constant danger, yet I couldn't figure out how to make my exit. Emotionally, I wanted to flee impulsively, but I understood it would only exacerbate matters. Therefore, I chose to stay and patiently wait for God's guidance and instructions. I prayed earnestly for protection, guidance, and direction, trusting in Psalm 121:1 _(my help cometh from the Lord)_.

As I mentally prepared myself to end this relationship, it dawned on me that I had been giving William too much power over my life. My fear was directed at him, not God. Consequently, the more evident it became that I wouldn't leave because I feared him, the more the relationship situation escalated. He insisted that we were bound together forever. After experiencing a spiritual renewal of my mind, a refreshing spirit enveloped me. I decided to turn my situation around and make God the focal point, bigger than any circumstance. I started to view God as my ultimate solution and my way of escape. As a result, my situation gradually diminished in size, and I regained control over my decision-making process. This freedom allowed me to step away from the stressful situation that had burdened me with high levels of anxiety and the fear of descending into a dark space of depression."

"You don't have to put on makeup, earrings, comb your hair, or dress up just to step out to the store. I love you just the way you are. I'm the only man who should be admiring my woman, anyway." This is what he would say whenever I had time off from work and wanted to relax at home or run errands like going to the grocery store or my favorite thrift shops. I'd respond, "I don't want to look like I don't care about myself, I'm not trying to impress anyone else; I just want to feel good about myself." "Where are you and your sisters or your girlfriends going to eat? Bring me something back, and make sure to call me before you leave the restaurant, so I can tell you what I want." This was his recurring request every time I made plans to spend time with my family or friends. I felt he was trying to control my time with loved ones.

"You're still at the nail shop? I thought you had an appointment. What's taking so long? I'm getting hungry. What are we having for dinner? Can you bring me something to eat?" These were his constant remarks whenever I tried to enjoy a relaxing day at the nail shop with my daughter, granddaughters, or sisters. I'd offer to leave the nail shop, to go grab something for him to eat, and then return to the nail shop to finish, but he would get upset, feeling that I was taking too long, spending my whole day in the nail shop. "You take too long getting dressed, combing your hair, and putting on makeup in the morning. You need to get up earlier and leave for work at 7:30 a.m. to beat the 8:00 a.m. traffic. You can be home by 3:30 p.m., so we can eat together by 4:00 p.m.". In his mind, this was a feasible daily routine and schedule for me. Sometimes, I would try to accommodate his time schedule, but I soon realized he was attempting to control me, therefore; I continued to take my time getting dressed and leaving the house at the time that I was ready to leave, so that I could maintain control of my own time, and set my own schedule.

This relationship felt suffocating, like being in jail. I had little control over my daily activities while living in his house. Everything was rushed, on a strict time limit, or scheduled. Laundry only on Saturday mornings before 10:00 a.m. to save on energy bills. Baths allowed only at night to keep the water bill low. Television had to be turned off after the 10:00 p.m. news, unless he stayed up late watching. Only one television could be on at a time to conserve energy. The window blinds could only be opened when he said so, to prevent excess sunlight from increasing the air-conditioning usage. He had sole control over the air-conditioning and decided when doors in the house could be closed. Reflecting on all this, I questioned whether this was the man I wanted to marry and spend my life with.

The Beginning of a New Relationship

Back in 2010, I had been unemployed for a while, so I was staying with my daughter when I first met William, shortly after getting back to work. We crossed paths at the grocery store. He was 10 years my senior; I was 45, and he was 55.

Dating an older man had always intrigued me. I believed older men were more stable and ready to settle down compared to those my age, who might still be playing around. During our first encounter, William appeared to be a Godly man regularly attending church, displaying a pleasant personality, exhibiting a peaceful behavior, and presenting himself well-groomed and mannered. He had been divorced for 12 years and was eager to find a life partner. I too, had gone through a divorce and had not been dating for about three years prior to meeting William.

After about three months of dating, William expressed his desire for me to be his woman and explained that he was not fond of casual dating; he wanted a wife. This aligned perfectly with my own thoughts about marriage, as I felt ready to give it another try. However, before committing to marriage, I wanted to sort out my own financial situation. Early retirement had taken a toll on my credit score, and I had accumulated delinquent bills during that time. Before meeting William, I had decided to move into a townhouse, and I was in the process of getting back on my feet. When I showed William the townhouse, he expressed that he believed we were meant to be together, as if it was God's plan. He didn't want me to live alone, and his conviction seemed genuine. Interestingly, I kept having dreams about him, which reinforced my belief that he was sent by a higher force. Moreover, everything that I dreamt about William seemed to materialize during the initial phases of our relationship.

William eventually proposed that I move into his house, and we would share the household expenses, allowing us to save money and get to know each other better as we worked towards marriage. This arrangement seemed reasonable and hopeful, considering the connection we felt and the dreams that had guided us. After praying about it, I decided to give the living arrangements with William a chance for one year. I made it clear to him that if we weren't progressing towards marriage within that time, I would find my own place. William agreed, and I retrieved my deposit from the townhouse and moved my clothes and belongings into his house. As I had given away my furniture, I didn't have much more to move.

However, soon after moving in, I noticed a change in William's behavior. Small things like the direction I put the tissue on the roll or how I folded bath towels led to arguments. He criticized my grocery shopping and cooking, even the way I held the steering wheel while driving. It felt like I couldn't ask him any questions without him feeling undermined, as he believed a woman should listen to her man without questioning him. I felt anxious and walked on eggshells, trying to avoid upsetting him. I knew every new relationship required effort, so I didn't want to give up too soon. Despite my efforts to appease him, and keep the peace in the house, arguments continued like clashes between two stubborn forces. The aftermath left me drained and overwhelmed. William would retreat to the other bedroom for days, not even speaking to me, and discarding my presence in his house. I began to feel an unpleasant, unhappy spirit in the house, and amongst William's inner spirit. One day, while William was away, I prayed and blessed every wall in the house with Blessed oil, hoping the Blessed oil would help to bring in a happier peaceful spirit.

William often blamed me for the turmoil in the relationship, stating that I wasn't listening to him, a situation he claimed he'd never experienced with his ex-wife, or in previous relationships, and he just couldn't understand why he was having such a hard time getting me to follow his rules. During these heated moments, I found myself behaving unlike my usual self, raising my voice, and becoming aggressive, which distressed me further. After making amends, we agreed not to argue anymore and tried to find solutions, but nothing seemed to work. Within three months, the petty arguments resurfaced.

I had never encountered such a tumultuous relationship in my previous marriages. Still, amidst the chaos, we had moments of laughter and deep conversations, discussing plans for a strong and lasting relationship. These pillow talks unveiled William's past struggles, revealing that his ex-wife had left him with the house note and depleted their bank account, leaving him in a state of distress. Listening to his side of the story, I became very skeptical about marrying him. I began to monitor our arguments. Paying close attention to the things that he said that I was doing wrong. He also told me that his wife was too in love with her sister, spending too much time with her, and wasn't giving him enough attention. Always blaming the women for the downfall of the relationship, appears to be his MO. I also noticed that William was not close to his family, therefore; it appeared that he was trying his best to isolate me from my family.

As time went on, I noticed that William was paying so much attention to me, trying his best to change me into the woman that he wanted me to be, that he could not focus on building our relationship. After every argument, William would tell me that I keep pushing our marriage date further, and further back. Eventually, the verbal confrontations using aggressive words, turned into physical altercations arising out of the arguments, to him laying on top of me to hold me down, and putting his hands around my neck nearly choking me, to stop me from talking, until I would tell him that I could not breathe, was the sign of a strong man molding his woman. After easing up off me, trying to kiss me, crying, and telling me he loves me, and he's sorry, he just needs his women to listen to him; he would always promise me that he would never put his hands on me again. Each time that we argued, William said that I made him put his hands on me. According to William, I would not listen to him. At first, the living arrangements worked for me, both of us were working, and I was able to save money, and pay off delinquent bills. After continuous petty arguments, the living arrangements soon went in left field. I kept threatening to leave his house, and he kept threatening to put me out of his house.

From Working to Retirement

Despite the challenges, I persisted in the relationship and tried my best to appease William, hoping to prevent further arguments. However, I soon realized that it wasn't me causing the chaos and confusion; it was him trying to exert control and change me. As a strong, independent woman, I refused to be controlled or lose my sense of self-worth, so I continued to be true to myself. In William's narrow, old-fashioned perspective, my refusal to be controlled was perceived as resistance, and he became frustrated because he couldn't mold me into the woman he desired—a weak, dependent partner. This ongoing struggle took a toll on both of us, leaving him grumpy, irritable, and unwilling to work. Initially, he had retired from a 30-year job and started a lawn care business with a considerable number of customers. However, I noticed a decline in his dedication to the business. When I inquired about it, he grew furious, refusing to discuss the matter.

Things took a turn for the worse, as William began to give up his business responsibilities and claimed to have handed most of his customers to his partner. His decision was driven by the belief that since I was living with him, he could fully retire. However, he didn't have the financial means to support a full retirement, and this led to constant financial strain. William started monitoring my every move, from the moment I woke up to when I left for work and returned home. It felt as if I was living life on his timeline. I felt rushed in everything I did.

Even after work, before I could even warm up my car, he would call to inform me that dinner was ready. My usual thrift shopping stops after work, which I found therapeutic, was cut short. I had to rush through everything to meet his expectations. If I made a stop at the thrift store and was even a few minutes late arriving home, he would call, expressing his impatience, stating that he was hungry, and the food was getting cold, or he was worried about me, so much is happing in the world, he wanted to make sure that I was okay, because he hadn't heard from me all day.

The stress and anxiety I experienced was becoming very overwhelming, as I felt like I was constantly walking on eggshells to avoid his anger aggression from surfacing. Tension was very tight in the house. It felt as if I made one wrong move, all hell would break loose, and we would argue and fight. I was right. One Friday, another petty matter arose, and we argued. He pointed his finger in my face yelling "shut up", and I tried my best to bite his finger off. He overpowered me and put his hands around my neck; he said to "calm me down." After he eased off me, while he went into the other room, I grabbed my purse and car keys, and ran out of the house to my sister's house. Hurrying to escape and backing out of the driveway doing 90 miles, he ran out of the house towards my car. I left everything behind and told myself that I would never return to his house again.

We Need to Get Married; Let's Set a Date

After leaving William's house, I felt very relieved. However, I was also emotionally unbalanced. I felt completely disoriented, discombobulated, unorganized, and homeless. I was an emotional wreck for a few days. However, after a day passed, I decided to answer his calls and accept his apologies. I knew that by doing so, he would allow me to return and retrieve my belongings. When I left his house during my emotional turmoil, I had only the clothes on my back and the shoes I was wearing. To get through the weekend, I went to Walmart, Goodwill, and City Thrift to buy some underwear, clothing, and shoes. I took a few days off from work to regain my emotional balance. During this time, I made a crucial decision to tell William that he would never lay a hand on me again. He understood that I didn't want to involve the police due to my job in law enforcement. Although I was living in a domestic violence situation, I feared the repercussions of being involved in a domestic violence situation. Despite my hesitation, I returned to the relationship, hoping that he would not resort to violence again. This time, however, I had a master plan. I had been able to save money in my savings account while sharing the house bills. Each pay period, I deposited $500 into my savings account, and I also managed to pay off old debts that were affecting my credit score.

Eventually, William proposed marriage, but I couldn't bring myself to give him an answer. He asked me to set a wedding date, claiming that God would bless our relationship and the chaos would if we were married. Although I hesitated, we agreed to get married on the anniversary of our relationship, and I shared the date with our family and friends. However, when the time came, neither of us mentioned anything about the wedding. I hadn't made any wedding plans because I was too busy plotting my final escape from the controlling relationship. As our anniversary date approached, I asked William about our wedding plans, and he denied ever agreeing to a date. He also claimed that I needed to "act right" before he would marry me. In his mind, acting right meant no questioning, just listening, and following along with whatever he told me to do. In my mind, I knew I had no intention of marrying William. In fact, I just needed to play along and make him think I did until I could find a way to escape and take my most valuable belongings with me.

As time went on, matters became worse in the relationship. It had gotten to the point that I was not able to make any decisions in the house that he said was our house. William did not want me to change the furniture around in the house. I could not decorate. He wanted to manage my paychecks, he wanted me to give him the house bill money, so that he could go pay the bills, therefore; I was not able to go pay the bills, not even the light bill unless he wasn't feeling well. Like clockwork, each payday, he started telling me to stop by the bank and get my portion of the house bill money contributions, put this amount in a money order, and bring the rest to him along with the money order. He started asking me for additional money, after I had already contributed my half on the house bills. If I told him that I was not giving him any more money, that I had already given him my contributions to the house bills, an argument would erupt, and we would go days without talking to each other.

William would ask me almost every day, "What are we eating for dinner"? If I decided on what to eat, he didn't want what I wanted. To avoid an argument, I ate what he ate. I felt myself falling into a dark headspace, leading to depression. I didn't have much of an appetite anyway, so it didn't really matter what I ate. If he heard me talking to my family or friends in person or on the phone, he would jump in the middle of our conversation and take over, trying to make me look small, and stupid, and make himself look big, like he knew it all. If I complained about him jumping in my conversation, an argument would erupt, and again, we would go days without talking to each other. At this point in the relationship, I was emotionally drained. I was so tired of the roller coaster rides with William. I was so ready to escape and leave all my clothes and belongings behind just to have a peace of mind. I realized that he was a very emotional man because he cried a lot.

Therefore, for my safety, I knew that I had to have a plan that would benefit me.

Over the entire time that we dated, William never bought me anything nice until he sensed that I was fed up and had lost interest in the relationship. Then he began to surprise me with inexpensive gifts and roses from his flower garden. He honestly thought that cooking dinner every day and rushing me home to eat by 4:30 p.m. was doing a good deed. Throughout the entire relationship, William was always broke; no money to travel, no money to save for a marriage, no money to build his business, no money to do much of anything. I soon realized that he was using me as his second source of income. As my mother used to say, the "straw that broke the camel's back" was when his truck broke down, and he was too broke to get another truck, or to get it fixed. He pretended that he did not need a vehicle because he said he really didn't go anywhere anyway. Therefore, he told me that he didn't want to put much money into getting his truck fixed. Instead, he wanted to drive my car. It got to the point that almost every day, he would be ready to jump in my car once I got to the house.

One day after dinner, he said he needed to ride around the corner. I decided to ask him, "what's around the corner, and why do you need to drive my car around the corner every day"? Once again, an argument erupted, and again, we went days without talking to each other. When I was sleeping, he would get in my car and take off without asking me if he could drive my car. An emotional wreck, I was becoming. I had made up my mind to finally escape this relationship. Putting his hands around my neck twice was the deal breaker for me. Driving my car was an ABSOLUTE NO, NO. I believed that every grown person needed their own vehicle, especially if they were driving without car insurance, as

William was driving. He said that he did not believe in paying unnecessary money out to insurance companies every month, making the rich richer, and keeping the poor man down. I did not mind sharing and giving in my relationship, but in this relationship, it was just too unbalanced. It looked like I was the only one sharing and giving, and he was always receiving.

Another "straw that broke the camel's back" was when he started complaining about my grandchildren coming over too much, turning his house into a daycare center, and them spending the night with me without asking him first. Getting in the way of me and my grandchildren was another ABSOLUTE NO, NO. I realized that I could not fight this battle alone. I started fasting and praying, asking God to guide and direct my footsteps, as well as my thinking. For safekeeping, I also started taking my valuable electronics, like one of my computers and my cameras, out of his house little by little when he was not watching me so closely and took them to my daughter's house. The relationship had become too overbearing, too toxic. I was afraid that if I stayed another year, I was going to end up dead, hurt in the hospital, or in jail for hurting or killing him. I felt in my spirit, it was time for me to GET OUT!

I Can't Live Here Anymore; I've Got to Escape

He began complaining about every little thing. When he was trying to sleep, and I was up watching TV, the volume was too loud. I had to turn the volume down to nearly 6 so he could sleep. Then, I couldn't hear the TV. When I was sleeping, he would have the TV volume up to over 20. If I asked him to turn the volume down, he would only close the door in the den, but I could still hear the TV in the bedroom. If I closed the bedroom door so that I wouldn't hear the TV, he would start an argument, yelling at me, saying this is his house, and not to close any doors in his house. I was so tired of arguing and fighting and running. Therefore, I would put earplugs in my ears so that I could go on to sleep with the TV volume up loud. Although we had three TVs in the house, only one TV could be on at a time. Being that it was his house, I was never hardly able to watch what I wanted to watch on TV, unless we were watching a movie together, I had to watch whatever he was watching, or find something to do on my computer.

I love the peaceful serenity of sitting near a window with the blinds open as I typed on the computer. Regardless of a rainy day or a sunny day, for some reason, sitting in front of the window with the blinds open, as I do my schoolwork on the computer, helped to ease my mind. It felt like a mindfulness meditation. I was able to stay focused on my classwork for hours at a time. One day I came to the house from work, and the window in the kitchen was blocked with a China cabinet. I asked why he blocked the window; he stated, "there is nothing to see out the window". Every time I opened the blinds in the bedrooms, to get in my mindfulness space, he would complain about the blinds being open, letting the sun in and sucking the air out of the house. Enough was enough. I was beginning to feel like I was in jail. I couldn't make any decisions on my own. I couldn't take it anymore. I was tired.

One weekend, William wrecked my nerves so badly that I left the house so fast without my purse. I had my phone in my hands and grabbed my keys off the key rack, jumped in my car, and locked the doors. Before I realized that I had left my purse with my billfold and bank card in it, he had locked the doors from the inside, causing my door key to not open the doors. I just went over to my daughter's house and stayed the weekend with no access to my backing account. I didn't even have my driver's license. I was so exhausted mentally and physically, I didn't care. I just wanted peace and rest. I slept and watched movies with my daughter and grandchildren until I fell asleep. William continued to call me every 30 minutes, asking me where I was, and what time I was coming home.

After spending the entire weekend at my daughter's house, I went back late that Sunday night. I heard the Holy Spirit speak to me and say, "silently and respectfully." When I went back to William's house, I eventually told him in a calm, respectful manner that I did not want to get married, and I was not going to play mind games with him any longer. I also told him that I was tired of helping him pay his house bills, and I was moving out of his house soon. I had built up enough strength and courage to face my fears of him trying to stand in my way of leaving for good.

Finding Peace in The Middle of The Storm

Quiet as kept, silently, I began searching for an apartment as I continued to pay off bills and rebuild my credit score. I was approved for a nice apartment, but there were no open units at the time; therefore, my name was added to the waiting list.

While on the waiting list, I contacted my real estate agent, and she got me approved to start house searching. I knew God had His hands on my situation because everything went so smoothly during my house searching. I also heard T.D. Jakes say, "When you're leaving a stressful situation, leave respectfully. Do not stop your normal routine." I heard Joel Osteen say, "Pick your battles, hold your tongue. Let God fight battles that are too big for you to fight alone." Therefore, without any hesitation or complaints, I continued my normal routine of working and contributing my half of the house bills, putting the money right in his hands, as he wanted me to do. Because I was so peaceful and humble, he thought that I was just mad when I told him that I did not want to get married, and that I was leaving soon, but I was serious as two heart attacks. Like R. Kelly says in his song, "When a woman is fed up, it's nothing a man can do." I was SO fed up. My mind had already escaped this relationship, but my body was still in the house.

Mentally, I was FREE! I was just waiting for the moment for God to tell me it was time to leave. Mentally, I was prepared to leave William's house with just my purse and my keys. Timing is everything when God has His hands on the wheel. So, I waited patiently for God's commands. I wanted to leave in peace, as well as in one piece. I felt as if I was in the middle of a tornado. I knew that I wanted to survive the storm. I also knew that I had to allow God to give me peace in the middle of my storm for me to survive and overcome.

One day, William was calculating bills. His light bill and mortgage taxes had increased. He decided to raise my portion of the house bill contributions. I did not want to provoke him into an argument, but I was curious; therefore, I asked him if he raised his portion of the bill contributions. As my mother used to say, "all hell broke loose." We argued for hours. He slept in the other bedroom. Although he said the increase was only for one month, it went on for months. William became so paranoid about the light bill that he didn't want any lights on in the house. If I was in the mirror combing my hair and decided to leave the bedroom and go to the bathroom, he would shout, "Turn that light out in the bedroom!" I would tell him, "I'm going right back in the bedroom."

It got to the point that I could not move around in the house and do much of anything without William complaining. William would complain if I turned the TV on in the bedroom while he was in the den watching the TV. If I stayed on my computer too long, he complained that I'm using too much electricity. On my off days, if I stayed up to watch late movies every

10 minutes, he would look in my face to see if I was asleep with the TV on, but he could stay up all night long with the TV on, often falling asleep with the TV on every night. He would tell me not to leave the TV on all night because the TV would burn out. If I was on my laptop computer, I would have to turn the computer off just to take a bathroom, stretch, or water break from the computer. Eventually, I broke down crying, and I told him that he was driving me crazy and was making me an emotional wreck.

He began smoking weed every day, saying that I was making his head hurt, and the weed was calming his nerves. I told William, "If I'm helping to pay the light bill in this house and helping to pay the house note, then I should be able to watch TV and use my computer when I want to. If I can't live in peace and harmony in my home, then I would not pay bills and live in a house with so much chaos and confusion." William became very quiet and stopped talking to me for weeks. I could feel that my time to escape the chaos and confusion was getting near. I knew me moving into my own house was in God's will because my house shopping went so smoothly. William didn't even know that I was house shopping. Most of my house viewings were during my lunch break, or I would leave work an hour early to view a house. I always made it to William's house right at 4:30 p.m. each time I viewed; therefore, he could not tell if I was telling the truth about buying a house or just bluffing.

Eventually, I found a house and paid for the appraisal and inspection on the house. Being very cautious not to provoke William into an argument, I was very hesitant about telling him that I had found a house and was moving out of his house soon. I continued to pray, asking God for a peaceful transition from his house to my house. As it got closer to my closing date, I informed William that I had found a house, and I had an upcoming closing date. For weeks, everything was quiet in the house. We barely said a word to each other. I began to pack my things in boxes and bins.

One day, he came to me in an aggressive tone asking me when my closing date was. I told him the closing date, but due to uncontrollable circumstances, I had to give him a second closing date, then a third closing date.

The third closing date set me back a whole month. William became very frustrated and frantic. He started panicking, telling me that I could not stay in his house for another full month, unless I was his woman. I told him that I would move my things into storage and live with my daughter until I closed on my house. At first, William was okay with me moving my belongings out of his house into storage.

Then he suddenly decided that I could stay there for the next month until my closing date. I told him that I would pay a prorated amount for that month because I would be moving by the middle of the month. I also told him that I would pay my portion of the light bill as well. We agreed to this arrangement. I continued to pray and pack.

The Final Escape

One Friday, I came into the house from work, and William was sitting in the den on the phone talking to his best friend about me leaving, how he was trying to help me save money by not moving my things into a storage room and staying with him. He continued to talk bad about me as if I wasn't in the house, telling his friend that I just suddenly decided to move out and break up our happy relationship. He went on and on about me breaking up our relationship. I was trying my best not to say anything. I just went into the bedroom and turned on my computer. I could feel my temperature rising. I held my tongue and didn't say a word, as long as I could. It was my payday, so I went back into the den, and put the bill money into his hands as he was talking on the phone to his friend. As I put the money in his hands, I said to William, "Here's your bill money. I would appreciate it if you would stop creating me out to be the bad person. Tell the truth, you need my help, that's why you do not want me to put my things in storage, storage is much cheaper than paying your mortgage." Then I turned and walked back into the bedroom.

William hurried and got off the phone, running into the bedroom, pushing me down on the floor, and pointing his finger in my face, hitting me upside my head and yelling, "This is my house. I can say whatever I want to say in my house." I yelled back at him to get up off me! I grabbed the nearest thing I could find, raising it to his face and told him, "that was the very last time he would ever put his hands on me". He got up crying and walked out of the room. We didn't talk any more that night. That Saturday morning, I got up and opened the blinds, and then got back into bed. I lay there in deep thought, staring out of the window feeling a peaceful serenity. William came into the bedroom, looking at my face and then out of the window, trying to see what I was looking at outside. He closed the blinds, saying the sun was making the house hot. I told him I wasn't looking at anything outside, I was in a daze, just thinking. He kept asking me what I was thinking about so hard. I didn't want to answer William because I knew it would start an argument and a fight. He wouldn't leave me alone. He kept saying, "a penny for your thoughts".

I knew that it would start an argument, but eventually, I told William what I was in deep thought thinking about. I started to cry, telling William how hurt and disappointed I was in him, how much I had helped him over the year, that we were together, and how I had tried to make the relationship work, but he was telling his family and friends that I was the bad person and the cause of our breakup. William started crying and laid on top of me, holding me down as I was lying in bed. I aggressively told him to get off of me, that I couldn't breathe, as I wiggled my way from under him and sat up in the bed crying. I noticed William was pacing back and forth, crying, and telling God, "This woman is going to make me kill her."

At that time, I heard the Holy Spirit say, "LEAVE NOW" very loudly. Therefore, I eased out of bed when William went into the bathroom and closed the door, crying and talking to God. I grabbed the t-shirt and leggings that I had laid out in case I had to run out of the house in the middle of the night, slipped on my tennis shoes, and grabbed my purse. I had started putting my keys in my purse at night. Keeping emergency clothes nearby and putting my keys in my purse were all part of my master plan for my final escape. I grabbed my computer and quietly left the house, driving to my daughter's house. 30 minutes later, I received a text message from William telling me not to come back to his house, he would call the police if I returned, and that he had changed the locks. I felt so relieved that I had finally escaped from living with William. I had no intentions of ever going back this time. It felt like a burden was lifted off me.

Although everything I owned, all my clothes, shoes, and belongings that I had neatly packed, were still inside William's house, I still felt so happy to be FRE! I knew this was the final escape. The Holy Spirit spoke to me and said, "Calm yourself, breathe, and rest. Do not call or text him in response to his text right now. Let him calm himself. In a few days, after he calms his nerves, he will let you get all your things". I was very obedient to the guidance and instructions of the Holy Spirit. Therefore, I waited patiently, as the Holy Spirit instructed me to do. I planned to call into work and use some vacation days because I had none of my clothes, shoes, makeup, or anything with me. I was going to purchase some more things in case he did not let me get some of my belongings before I went back to work.

That Sunday morning, William texted and told me that I could come and get some of my clothes and shoes for work. He also said that he would text me with a date to pick up all my other belongings later, as he had to clear his mind and calm his nerves before that date. I'm very thankful that I have a relationship with God, which allows me to hear from the Holy Spirit. Being able to hear from the Holy Spirit gave me guidance and instructions during a duress situation. Receiving guidance and instructions from the Holy Spirit is what helped me to escape without getting hurt and ending up in the hospital, or worse, in my grave. Had I allowed my emotions to overpower my thinking and lead me out of this mentally, physically, and financially abusive relationship, it could have possibly created a more violent situation.

Most women choose to stay in abusive relationships because they are afraid to leave for various reasons. Many women may try to escape, but they may not make it out alive. Thank God, I made it out alive. I knew one wrong move, me saying one wrong word, could have provoked William to harm me, out of his anger emotion becoming off balanced. I remember hearing T.D. Jakes say, "When surviving isn't safe, focus on surviving". Leaving an unsafe situation, you might have to leave something behind. Therefore, I was hoping and praying that I was able to make a safe and peaceful transition. I was hoping and praying that I was able to take all my things with me. However, my focus was on surviving. If I had to leave everything behind, then so be it, as long as I survived.

I DRESS UP MY PAIN
(PART ONE)

ROSALIND MILES

In today's world, many young women haven't been fortunate enough to experience genuine love or authenticity, either from family or friends. Rosalind Miles, born in Chicago, Illinois, is the cherished daughter of the late Frank and Cora Miles and an alumna of Bremen High School.

In 2007, Rosalind made the move to Memphis, TN, seeking a path towards greater success. This decision led her to the welcoming arms of the Pursuit of God Transformation Center, shepherded by Senior Pastors Ricky and Sheila Floyd.

Within this congregation, Rosalind immersed herself in several ministries – Evangelism, Security Armor Bearer, Children, and Intercessory Prayer – each playing a pivotal role in her personal transformation.

Rosalind is not just deeply spiritual; she's entrepreneurial as the proud owner and CEO of Magnificent Hands Cleaning Services. A mother to ten wonderful children, she takes immense pride in her family. Today, she continues to call Memphis, TN her home.

DEDICATION

This initial chapter, "Part One" of the Anthology, is lovingly dedicated to my beloved late Mother, Cora Miles, and my cherished children: MarKida, Andre, Antionette, Corrie, Michelle, Michael, Cheryl, Dominique, Tierra, and Shaniqua. I extend my deep gratitude to my Pastor, Ambassador Ricky D Floyd, who prophetically guided me and encouraged my journey into writing. Above all, my utmost dedication is to my Savior, The Almighty God, for His healing touch and salvation.

I DRESS UP MY PAIN
(PART ONE)

This is my story of how I overcame my pain of drug, emotional and verbal abuse. I dressed it up and I blocked out things that were hurting and hindering me in my life. (Psalm 91).

Hi, I'm Rosalind, but some people call me Lady. I'm the proud mother of ten amazing children. Before I reached the point where I am today, I had to overcome some past pain and struggles. However, God provided me with strength (Psalm 23:3). I concealed my pain behind a smile, and no one knew what I was holding inside—both happiness and anger.

I was born in Chicago, Illinois to the late Frank and Cora Miles, and I am incredibly proud to say that. My father wasn't around long enough to show me how love should be expressed and how a man should treat a woman. Unfortunately, my favorite man, the only significant male figure in my life at that time, passed away when I was nine years old. I couldn't comprehend why God would take away my favorite person instead of my father. So, while I grew up attending church, I didn't understand the concept of having a personal relationship with God or the effort it required. Despite being daddy's girl, I harbored anger towards those around me.

Then, God blessed me with an amazing Queen named Cora, who raised me. My mother was the best mother in the world to me. I made sure to tell her that if I turned out to be a bad person, it wasn't her fault. She fulfilled her role as a parent and raised me well. I thought my mom was a wealthy lady because we never lacked anything a child could want or need. She shielded us from witnessing her struggles. I had four incredible brothers and three amazing sisters. Their names are Andre, Robin, Michael, Benjamin, Terrance, Cheryl, and Ida. My mother exemplified genuine love and did her utmost to protect us. We lived in various neighborhoods, ranging from the Westside to the Southside.

I don't have many memories of my dad except he was very abusive to my mother and used drugs. He would come home from the bar drunk and high on drugs and start fighting my mother for no reason. He was also verbally abusive to her. I remember waking up seeing my dad chasing my mother around the dining room table calling her bad words. I also told him when I get big, I am going to beat you up for fighting my mother. Although I had decided I would beat him up, it did not happen because he suddenly passed away from a drug overdose. My mother went on and continued to live her life raising eight children as a single parent. She loved to travel. I love to travel as well. Every summer when school was out we went somewhere out of town.

At the age of ten, I distinctly recall living in the Cabrini Green Projects, where the Black Stone Rangers and the Black Panthers were present. It was a challenging environment where you had to be prepared to defend yourself. Fortunately, I didn't have to worry because my older sister handled all the fighting, and she was absolutely fierce when it came to protecting our family. Eventually, we relocated to the Robert Taylor Projects, specifically to 4022 S State Street, Apartment 1301, situated on the 13th floor. It was there, I experienced a family male friend touching me inappropriately. This was wrong because he was a grown man and I was a child. I was afraid to say anything to anyone because he told me if I said anything he would kill me and my mother.

Living in the projects there was always a lot of fighting, so we decided to move. Family was important to us, and everyone looked out for each other. However, big families always challenged other big families in the projects often because it was eight of us. Interestingly, the older three siblings were the ones who excelled in fights; they emerged victoriously every time.

Eventually, we relocated to Harvey, Illinois, and I enrolled at Brian Elementary School on 147th Broadway. Life started to improve during my 8th-grade year, but we ended up moving once again. This time, we settled in Morgan Park, specifically the Racine Quarts area. I attended John Shoop School and graduated from 8th grade. It was a fun time, but I still found myself involved in fights because anger still lingered within me. Family disputes were frequent, and it seemed like each one of us carried some form of resentment.

We moved once more, returning from Morgan Park back to Harvey, Illinois. At that point, I began attending Bremen High School in Midlothian, Illinois.

Unfortunately, I found myself getting into fights once again.

I was forced to have sex with a man I thought was my family member. After one time I got pregnant. Indeed, at the age of 15, I found myself pregnant and gave birth to a beautiful baby girl when I was 16. As a result, I experienced a whirlwind of emotions—I felt hurt, angry, confused, ashamed, rebellious, and embarrassed. It was during this time that I began to conceal my pain behind a façade, an act I referred to as **"Dressing Up My Pain."** I kept my pregnancy a secret from everyone because I felt deep shame and hurt. So, I carried on with my life, keeping this burden to myself.

The thought of revealing the truth to my brothers terrified me. I was apprehensive about how they might react, as it could lead to negative consequences. My mother was extremely protective of us, but surprisingly, she felt comfortable with the idea of us visiting this person or place. Here's what happened. It was dark and he came upstairs in the room I was in, got in the bed with me. I started to scream, however no one was there to hear me, and he put his hand over my mouth. The rest was history. I was very angry afterwards and I thought it was my fault. Shortly after, I started to feel different in my body. I couldn't explain it but I was going through changes without knowing. Well my mother and aunties noticed the changes and plotted to get me checked. They knew but my "auntie" took me to the health department for a pregnancy test. Yes, it was positive. I wondered, what do I tell my "auntie" when she asks what the doctor said? When she did ask, my response was, "he said I have a cold." I remembered feeling embarrassed, like I had let my mother and myself down. Now what do I tell my mother and auntie when they ask who the father is? What do I tell him? So, I lied and they believed I had a cold.

My aunt was nosey, so she went and asked the doctor herself how many weeks pregnant was I? I dropped my head in shame. To make a long story short, I gave birth to an amazing baby girl that makes me smile while writing this story. Many people wanted me to get rid of her, but "she was all in God's plan", in Pastor's voice. As it reads in Psalms 91, He is the protector.

Children are gifts from God. After finding out I was pregnant, I dressed up my pain and continued to live my life the best I could. I realized, she was my blessing from God that came out of a terrible situation but I was also angry, bitter and confused.

Growing up, I carried this anger and pain because I didn't talk to anyone about my abuse. I internalized my feelings and what I was going through. At this point, I was still bitter. I kept all that had happened to me to myself and moved forward with my life. My amazing mother, along with my sisters and brothers, helped me raise my daughter, and to this day, I'm grateful to them. I was still out of my mind and angry. By the time I was 29, I had ten amazing children: MarKida, Andre, Antoinette, Corrie, Michelle, Michael, Sheryl, Dominique, Tierra, and Shaniqua. They're all still my babies. I love them so deeply that their pain is my pain. I began having children every other year or even a year apart. I was seeking love in my children, knowing they'd love me back the way I loved them. At 16, I did things I shouldn't have. The bullying I faced at ages 12 and 13 was horrible. I kept it to myself, but it hurt. I tried to show people the love I wished for, always looking for friends. My mother once told me, "there are no friends," and I later realized she was right. I felt a void, perhaps something missing from my relationship with my siblings. Our love for each other was challenging. The saying "hurt people hurt people" rang true for me. I didn't have a relationship with God to understand my hardships. Going to church, I naively thought I'd go to heaven just by being there. I harbored a lot of resentment growing up. Searching for a love to fill the void left by my father, I sought it in men, a mistake. The speed at which I had children surprised even me. Growing up with four boys and four girls, our household of eight was filled with differing attitudes and personalities. Life was rough.

Seeking a fresh start, I moved to my first apartment at 18. By the ages of 19 or 20, I relocated to San Diego, CA to be near my brother, who was stationed with the Marines. With four children, I tried to fit into life there, even meeting an older lady who lived in the same apartment complex. My brother helped me settle in, but soon after, he moved his family back to Chicago and was deployed overseas. His absence stung. Feeling alone, I unfortunately found myself with the wrong crowd, thinking they were right for me.

These people were much older than me. I was not aware at the time but most of them were addicted to drugs. It is how I met my twin's father. He was a big time drug dealer from Los Angeles. He took good care of me and my children, and I found myself involved in his world, even selling his drugs. He had a chop shop in LA, and I had the freedom to drive any car I fancied. I hung around with older folks, and on a particular Friday night, on the way to a club with my neighbor, things took a turn. I was 24 by then and could finally get into clubs. During a brief stop at her house, she asked if I had any "work" with me. To her surprise, I did, and she wanted to buy some. After the sale, as she indulged herself in the kitchen, my mind was set on heading to the club. That evening marked my introduction to cocaine. I didn't feel its effects initially but soon found myself chasing the high she so clearly felt. My partner was a significant supplier, oblivious to the fact that I had started using. My consumption grew, especially after my brother's departure, leaving me feeling increasingly isolated. The people who claimed to love me seemed to constantly let me down. As my addiction worsened, I became pregnant yet again. The men in my life, whom I mistakenly believed loved me, never stayed. Friends seemed to use me, and the relationship with my twins' father became tumultuous. There was an alarming incident where he attempted to kidnap our twins, which escalated into a confrontation with the police. Thankfully, I got my twins back.

Seeking solace, I began attending church with my brother, who had become a minister. Reverend Jones taught me a scripture, "I can do all things through Christ, who strengthens me," which became my anchor in stormy times. But old habits die hard. Despite the spiritual upliftment, I continued using and surrounded myself with the wrong crowd. Another pregnancy followed, and I gave birth to a beautiful baby girl. My life felt chaotic. I decided to move from San Diego, CA to Greenville and Leland, MS, where most of my family resided. I attempted to restart things with the twins' father, but it was futile. Every time, I found the strength to move on from stressful and abusive relationships.

I had two of my beautiful daughters there. I put my best foot forward with living in Mississippi. It was different from what I was used to. At this point in my life, I was tired of getting high. One night, I ran some bathwater, took off my clothes, got down on my knees by the tub, raised up my arms high and said, "Lord, you said ask and I shall receive". I proceeded to take my bath. I have tried to stop many times but I wanted this time to be different. I got in the bathwater and didn't realize God was washing it away. This time it was different. So different that I put the crack I came home with in the garbage where I could not go back and get it. It was a year later that I realized I had been clean since that day. The devil said I would never stop using drugs, but we know the devil is a liar. So I'm still trying to live in Mississippi.

Life in Memphis, TN was a slower pace than I was used to, but it's where I truly discovered God, realizing He had always been within me. Growing up, I believed that just attending church was a ticket to heaven. Now, I feel I truly know God as my father. When I first moved to East Memphis, Sundays were dedicated to searching for a church home. Though I tried many, none of the churches resonated with me. My nephew, who was already a resident of Memphis, suggested a church close to my Thrift Street residence, the Pursuit of God Transformation Center. He said, "Auntie lady, are you looking for a church? I know one you will like, and I stand on that." He said, "Pastor Ricky Floyd is the truth". He held Pastor Ricky Floyd in high regard, claiming him to be genuine. On my first visit there in 2008 after relocating to Frayser, Pastor Ricky gave me the nickname "Chicago Red," which stuck. As promised by my nephew, I felt something profound in that church. Soon, Sundays and Wednesdays were reserved for worship. Despite initially sitting at the back, the warmth and love from the congregation were unmistakable. Church became my sanctuary. No longer under the grip of addiction, I invested my time in serving the Lord and embracing Psalms 91, slowly healing from past pains.

My involvement deepened at Pursuit of God. The church was my new haven; it provided a sense of family. I joined multiple ministries. First, the drama ministry, participating in five plays. Then, the evangelism team, where we took our message to the streets, prayed for strangers, and visited nursing homes to offer encouragement and prayer. The joy in the elders' eyes was evident when we shared gifts with them. My commitment grew as I joined the security team and became an armor bearer. Each role refined my understanding of God, molding me towards the ultimate aim of total transformation.

Indeed, stepping into the Pursuit of God Transformation Center ensures change will take place. Here, I learned how to address and heal from my past traumas. Fasting, praying, and serving with the intercessor team taught me to conquer my fears, foster unity, and support one another. Harboring no grievances, understanding that God is everything. With serenity, I've learned to accept things beyond my control, influence where I can, and discern the difference between the two. This is just the beginning of my journey in addressing my pain.

FACING THE COMPLICATED TRUTH

JENAE BAKER

Jenae Baker is a Long Beach, California native and has been a successful Christian wife for over 20 years. She is well-known for her passion for praying and intercession, and is committed to her local congregation for prayer. Together with her husband, she runs several successful businesses that are growing steadily. Jenae is the author of two books, "Kiss My Past and Put Me In The Game Coach", both of which are available for purchase. Her greatest joy comes from being a nurturing mother to three amazing young adult children, and she holds faith, family, and friends in high regard.

If you're looking to connect with Jenae, coaching and entrepreneurship are some key areas where you can find your purpose and passion. She has studied and mastered the faith of sowing, along with many other Godly principles. This book anthology is just one of many that she will continue to author.

DEDICATION

I dedicate this story to God first, for giving me the strength, courage, and another opportunity to share my testimony publicly. God's faithfulness and His truth are unwavering. As Romans 8:28 says, all things work together for the good of those who love God and are called according to His purpose. I am grateful to God for using my experiences to bless not only me but also countless others.

I also dedicate this to my parents, Robert and Christy, who have loved me, believed in me, and supported me throughout my healing process.

To my husband, Julius, thank you for showing me that good, wholesome people still exist. Your presence has been a safe haven for me and our children.

FACING THE COMPLICATED TRUTH

All I could smell was the smell of Bengay as I hysterically screamed, "No Paw Paw, stop Paw Paw, I promise I won't tell anyone". In the far back bedroom of my maternal grandmother's big beautiful home located in Carson, California is where I experienced some of the most horrific times of my early childhood. It all began in 1985 when I was just three years old – yes, three. My mother went into labor with my youngest brother, resulting in a complicated delivery and an extended stay in the hospital. While she was there, I found myself under the primary care of my grandmother, who I affectionately called "Mema," and her husband, whom I lovingly referred to as "Paw Paw." Paw Paw, my step-grandfather, was a retired vet, always at home during the daytime. When Mema worked as a high school teacher, I attended daycare from 8:00 a.m. until noon most days. However, the rest of the time, it was just me and Paw Paw. He would pick me up from daycare and babysit me until my grandmother returned from work.

Paw Paw was a remarkable man, standing at about 5 feet and 10 inches tall, with a slender frame and curly hair. Despite the age gap between him and my grandmother, he took exceptional care of their home, ensuring it was always clean and organized. He even excelled in the kitchen, handling most of the cooking duties. As I spent those days with him, I grew to appreciate his presence and the bond we shared during my Mema's absence.

He & my grandmother slept in two separate bedrooms and he would always lure me into his bedroom with candy and potato chips. Every afternoon he would give me candy and turn a cartoon on the television for me to watch. He used the cartoon on the television as a distraction while he would take advantage of me. This grown elderly man would stick his tongue in my mouth and kiss me as I cringe with disgust. I could feel his long wet nose hairs on the top of my lip. I couldn't wait for it to be over so I could wipe his disgusting saliva from my face. I would tell him "Paw Paw, that's nasty. I don't like you kissing me" He would say, "It is not nasty, little girl. You are my baby doll and this is how I kiss my baby doll". From that point, he would undress me while offering me more and more candy and potato chips. This man would literally kiss and lick every part of my body including my under arms and my feet. I was a very ticklish child and he enjoyed making me laugh and swarm, but I hated it. Nothing about this was fun or funny to me. I would desperately beg him to stop but he would only stop long enough to say he was going to whoop me if I did not shut up. He even said that baby dolls don't talk. He compared me to baby dolls so much that as I got older I found myself not liking baby dolls at all. I would cry when people gave them to me as a gift and would throw them in the corner of my closet. I would tell my step Paw Paw that I was going to tell my grandmother & mother what he was doing to me when they weren't around. He would threaten to have both of his dogs bite and kill me, my mother, my brother and my grandmother if I told anyone what he was doing to me. Oftentimes he would go outside in the backyard and bring his dogs in the bedroom just to scare me. He would restrain me and let his dogs jump on me and lick me while he laughed at me. He had two big and hairy German shepherds. They obeyed his voice and he knew without shadow of doubt that I was terrified of them but he did it anyway. This abuse and molestation went on for years.

One night at our home I was sleeping in the bed with my mother when she woke me up abruptly from a nightmare about what Paw Paw had been doing to me. She asked me what was wrong? I didn't know what she was talking about. She looked worried and confused as she proceeded to tell me that I was talking in my sleep saying, "No, Paw Paw. Stop Paw Paw". I couldn't believe that those words came out of my mouth as I have been trying so hard to keep the abuse a secret.

I was so afraid and ashamed to tell her what he had been doing to me, so I kept insisting that it was just a bad dream. She wasn't buying it, though. She asked me over and over again, but I refused to speak. Despite my silence, she sensed that something had happened to me. In a determined effort, she asked me to put on my shoes and jacket, waking up my brother and getting him dressed as well. Without delay, we drove fifteen minutes to my father and step-mother's apartment.

My father has always been an excellent listener and skilled at asking questions. He's also incredibly persistent, and my mother knew that if anyone could get the truth out of me, it would be him. With great care and concern, he started questioning me about what I had been saying in my sleep. He offered me juice and warm hugs, repeatedly reassuring me that I could share anything with him without fear of harm. He wanted me to feel safe.

Though I desperately wanted to believe him, I still couldn't bring myself to open up completely. I kept insisting that there was nothing to tell, that it was just a bad dream. But my father persisted, asking more questions, and finally, with trembling and fear in my voice and heart, I disclosed to him, my mother, and my stepmother what Paw Paw had been doing to me.

The revelation left them stunned, tears filling their eyes as they hugged me and apologized profusely. They made sure to let me know that they believed me and that everything would be alright. My mother's anger erupted, and she called him all sorts of curse words and perverts in her emotional reaction. She even recalled how he would call her his bedroom when she was a little girl telling her to bring him water with his private parts showing. The more she talked about him the more upset she became. She started shaking and biting her lip. I begged my mother to calm down. I asked her, my dad and my stepmother not to say anything because I did not want Paw Paw or his dogs to hurt us but my mother said we had no choice but to let Mema know what was going on.

My mother, my brother, and I headed over to my Mema & Paw Paw's house while my mom cried, asking God why this had happened to her baby throughout the entire car ride. My dad and stepmother stayed back at home. When we arrived at my Mema's house, it was evident that we had woken her up, as it was the middle of the night, and she took quite some time to come to the door. She opened the door with anger, cursing and yelling at us for disturbing her sleep, reminding us that she had to work in the morning. Despite her irritation, she noticed my mom crying and asked us what was wrong. My mom yelled at her and said, "What's wrong is your sick disgusting perverted husband that's what's wrong!" She then told my grandmother that he had been molesting me.

My grandmother looked surprised and upset. She did not want to believe what she had heard. She asked me to tell her exactly what he did to me. She kept making me repeat it but as I was telling her she kept interrupting me, telling me to speak up and accusing me & my mom of lying on him. She told me my Paw Paw loved me and would never ever do anything to hurt me or any of us. She accused my mom of putting me up to the "accusations" but I kept telling her that wasn't true. She yelled in my face and told me not to ever say that about her husband again or she would beat the skin off of me. She also stated that he has a full grown woman like herself. What could he possibly want with an "ugly little girl like me!" My poor little heart was breaking. She called my Paw Paw from the back room and asked him if he was molesting me? Of course he denied it. He even went so far to say that if he had ever touched me inappropriately let the Lord make him crippled before he died.

My mother started calling him a child molesting pervert. She even started to swing and hit him. My grandmother became extremely upset with us and forcefully pushed us out of her home in the middle of the night. She told us that if we didn't leave she would call the police on us and have both of us charged with defamation of character. I didn't have a clue what that meant. My Paw Paw was standing behind her saying he was going to sick his dogs on me because I was a bad girl. It was awful. We had caused so much commotion that the neighbors began to come out of their home asking what was going on. It felt like the worst night ever. My mother started telling everyone what Paw Paw did. It was humiliating.

My grandmother didn't speak to us for months but it felt like forever and we were definitely not welcomed in her home or anywhere around her home. Even though my grandmother worked and made decent money her husband was considered to be wealthy and he was a great financial provider. She wasn't going to let anyone come and interfere with the financial stability of her household. I felt so bad. I felt like the distance between us and them was all my fault. My mother had to get doctors and police involved. Paw Paw eventually agreed to take a lie detector test. In the middle of the test my mother said he started complaining about chest pains and believed he faked a heart attack because he was failing the lie detector test.

Meanwhile my mother was so devastated about what her stepfather had been doing to me that she began hanging out with people in our neighborhood and before long she began using cocaine, quickly becoming addicted to it. Once my grandmother found out that my mom was using drugs, she started back talking to us and allowing us in her home. Thank God I was never left alone again with her husband.

Sometimes my grandmother would get drunk and physically attack Paw Paw in front of me. She would tell me she was beating him up for touching me inappropriately. I would cry because I felt sorry for him but once she sobered up she would say things like, "you know your Paw Paw loves you and he would never do anything to hurt you." He would smile and wink his eye at me or blow me a kiss while she wasn't looking at him. In the meantime my mother's addiction was getting worse. She started getting physically abused in front of us by different drug dealers for owing them money. She would get high and talk to me like I was her therapist. She would cry and tell me things that she was going through with different people.

When someone would knock on our door, my brother and I would hide under the bed. One evening when I was in the first grade my mother forgot to pick me up from school. It had gotten dark and I was the only child outside waiting to be picked up. I thought my mother had been beaten to death. I was afraid. It just so happened that a janitor was working late and noticed that I was still there. He called the police and I was taken to the police precinct until my father came and picked me up. He told the police that my mother was battling an addiction and that I would be staying with him for a while. I stayed with my dad and stepmother for a little while but eventually ended up back at home with my mother and brother. I was going to my grandmother's house frequently and she started teaching me how to pray for my mother. I would have to repeat after her and learn to read Psalm 23. I would ask her why I have to pray and she would tell me that God listens to children. Not only was my mother delivered from cocaine my grandmother was also delivered from alcoholism. God is faithful.

Time passed, and as we both grew older, Paw Paw's mobility began to decline. He would call out for my brother and me to bring him water and food. In an act of defiance for the pain he had caused me, I sometimes put his water in dirty cups.

Despite spending nights at their home, I always made sure to sleep in the front bedroom with my grandmother, finding solace in her presence and feeling safe once again.

When I turned seven, Paw Paw had a terrible fall, breaking his legs. Sadly, his legs never healed, and not long after, he passed away. I recall his earlier statement about being crippled by the Lord if he touched me inappropriately. While I can't say that the Lord made him crippled, it was an eerie coincidence that he became crippled before his death.

My mother allowed me to miss his funeral to attend a school party. Two years after his passing, we moved to Tennessee, and life took a positive turn. It felt like a fresh start for us. My mother began working full-time, and my grandmother bought us a home, granting me the luxury of having my very own bedroom for the first time. I believe my grandmother was in a better position financially after her husband's death, allowing her to retire and travel extensively. She took me along on her journeys to places like Puerto Rico, Spain, and various states within the United States. We would go on shopping sprees together, and she made sure I never lacked anything financially. I felt incredibly fortunate, even though material possessions didn't matter much to me. Throughout all this, Paw Paw was never a topic of conversation.

When I turned sixteen, my grandmother surprised me by getting me a car against my mother's wishes. I couldn't have been happier about it. My grandmother began being extremely generous towards me. I did not understand why until one night while she was drunk, she called me and my mother. During the call, she admitted to being raped by brother when she was a teenager. She told us that she became pregnant as a result of her the rape and was fifteen when she had her first child.

Her mom did not believe her which is why she chose not to believe me. Her anger towards me was because of her experience.

Often, we find ourselves tempted to judge situations without understanding their underlying causes. In a significant moment, God granted me compassion and insight into my grandmother's life. She had been burdened with a secret, carrying the weight of shame for decades. When a similar situation occurred to me, involving someone she loved, she reacted in a way mirroring her mother's response. This revelation helped me comprehend why she turned to heavy drinking and became aggressive. Thankfully, God's faithfulness shone through as she found the strength to speak her truth. Witnessing her transformation not only improved her life but also had a profound impact on mine.

My grandmother and I developed an incredibly close and loving relationship. We could openly discuss anything and everything, and she bestowed valuable Godly wisdom upon me. She emphasized the significance of entrepreneurship and property investment, always encouraging me to speak my truth regardless of others' beliefs. In fact, she even urged me to write a book.

Today, I am happily married for twenty years, with four adult children. We raised our kids in the word of God, and He has protected them from adverse childhood experiences. We now own multiple businesses, and I take pleasure in sharing my testimony of turning adversity into opportunity.

Looking back at the pain I endured with my step-grandfather, I choose to see it as an opportunity for my grandmother to embrace her truth. It was also a chance for me to teach my children and others that when something feels wrong, it likely is, and they should never hesitate to confide in us, their parents. Some family members playfully teased me for not keeping secrets, but I believe that when I held on to those painful secrets, the abuse persisted. Once I found the courage to speak up, the abuse finally stopped. After all, water was never meant to be held; it was meant to be walked on.

Final Thoughts and Facts About Sexual Abuse

- No one deserves to be abused.
- In most cases, the abusers are someone that you know and trust.
- If you were forced or coerced to engage in any sexual activities you didn't want to, it is sexual abuse. "No" means "No".
  Child molesters often engage children in inappropriate sexual interactions gradually and playfully. As a result, children may enjoy their attention and not object to the ongoing abusive activities. This is still sexual abuse and is not the child's fault no matter how they respond to the abuse.
- Every Ninety Eight Seconds, someone in the United States is sexually assaulted.

OVER—COMING LIFE OBSTACLES

CHALISSA HOUSTON

I was born on May 22, 1970, in Memphis, TN, to my loving parents, Freddie and Sandra Houston. Growing up, I had the joy of being part of a large family with seven siblings; tragically, we lost one brother along the way. My educational journey began at Northside High School, where I dedicated myself to my studies, proudly graduating in 1989. However, my thirst for knowledge didn't stop there. I also spent many years attending South Parkway Church of God in Christ, finding nourishment for my soul through faith and a close-knit community. Later, I embarked on a new chapter by enrolling at the Healthcare Training Institute, located in the heart of Midtown on Union Ave.

Throughout my personal growth, I aspired to be an independent young woman. Despite the challenges of being a teenage mother, my determination to provide a stable and nurturing environment for my children never waned. This drive motivated me to achieve a significant milestone: completing my healthcare training. I didn't just obtain one certification, but four—Medical

Assistant, Dialysis Technician, and Certified EKG Monitor Technician—which opened doors to new opportunities in the healthcare field. For an impressive 13 years, I dedicated my expertise and compassion to Methodist Hospital, making a meaningful impact as a valued employee. However, my heart always prioritized the well-being and education of children.

Fueled by passion, I accomplished another monumental goal. 32 years ago, I realized my dream of purchasing a home. But I didn't stop there. I transformed my home into not just a haven for myself but also a daycare center. After obtaining certifications in CDA and TECTA and becoming licensed by the Department of Human Services, I made it my mission to create a safe and loving space for children. My dedication led to becoming a successful business owner, operating two childcare centers, and giving countless children a place to grow, learn, and play. What was once a personal sanctuary has become one for many children, thanks to my care.

OVERCOMING LIFE OBSTACLES

While growing up, I experienced a noticeable contrast in the values and perspectives within our community. Our neighborhood had lower crime rates, and the presence of involved parents played a vital role in shaping our lives. Our parents held the role of decision makers, guiding us with their wisdom and unconditional love. Instead of being consumed by electronic devices, we spent our days outdoors, immersing ourselves in the wonders of the world.

One of the highlights of my weekends was participating in church activities. Attending church had a special place in my heart. Also being a part of the Sunshine Band and Purity Group brought me immense joy. I come from a large family, with seven brothers and one sister. My father served as a Pastor, and my mother was devoted to missionary work within the church for many years. The impact of my mother's influence on my life cannot be overstated. During the challenging moments I encountered, my mother stood as my unwavering supporter. She consistently instilled in me the belief in myself and reminded me of the limitless possibilities that awaited me. I share her sentiments with you: have faith in yourself and trust in the power of God. When you hold unwavering belief, all things become attainable.

Born on May 22, 1970, in Memphis TN, to my loving parents, Freddie and Sandra Houston. Growing up I had the joy of being part of a large family with seven siblings, although we tragically lost one brother along the way.

My educational journey began at Northside High School, where I dedicated myself to my studies and proudly graduated in 1989. However, my thirst for knowledge did not stop there. I also spent many years attending South Parkeay Church of God in Christ, where I found nourishment for my soul through faith and a close-knit community. Later on, I embarked on a new chapter of my life by enrolling at the Healthcare Training Institute, located in the heart of Midtown on Union Ave.

Throughout my personal growth, I always aspired to be an independent young woman. Despite the challenges of being a teenage motor, my determination to provide a stable and nurturing environment for my children never wavered. It was this drive that motivated me to achieve a significant milestone in my life—completing my healthcare training. Graciously. I obtained not just one, but four certifications as a Medical Assistant, Dialysis Technician and Certified EKG Monitor Technician, which opened doors to new opportunities in the healthcare field.

For an impressive 13 years, I dedicated my expertise and compassion to Methodist Hospital, where I made a meaningful impact as a valued employee.

However, my heart always held a special place for the well being and education of children. Fueled by my passion, I set out to accomplish another monumental goal. 32 years ago, I realized my dream of pursuing my own home. But I didn't stop there, I transformed my home into a nurturing environment, not just for myself, but also as a daycare center for children. I also obtained certifications in CDA and TECTA and became licensed by the Department of Human Services.

Creating safe and loving space for little ones to thrive became my mission.

My dedication to children's well being led me to become a successful business owner. Now, proudly owns and operates two children centers, providing countless children with the opportunity to grow, learn, and play. My home which was once my personal haven, has transformed into a sanctuary for these little ones, thanks to my unwavering care.

My story stands as a testament to perseverance and the pursuit of dreams. Through my spirit, I aim to inspire others to overcome obstacles and make a positive impact. Today, I celebrate myself, Chalissa Houston, embodying strength, resilience, and a profound love for children's futures.

On a fateful Friday in 1986, my life changed dramatically. At sixteen, I discovered I was pregnant. Overwhelmed with fear and uncertainty, I grappled with when and how to share this news. I confided in my sister, understanding I couldn't keep such a secret for long. The subsequent shame from those around me was heart-wrenching. Facing judgment and condemnation, my pastor, whom I had sought for guidance, swiftly relegated my mother and me to the church's back pews, hidden from the congregation. In that moment, I realized the profound impact of my situation on myself, my parents, and our church family.

I distinctly recall expressing to God that despite everything, including my upbringing in the church, I hadn't abandoned my faith. Amid challenges like adhering to religious practices, fasting, praying, and giving tithes, I found solace in a heartfelt conversation with God. Humbly, I sought forgiveness, even if it wouldn't come from my church. To my surprise, a profound tranquility enveloped me. It was during this introspective exchange that I realized I had a choice regarding my church affiliation. I saw that God's love, demonstrated through my mother, was greater than any religious institution or set of rules.

It became vital to understand that I am not solely defined by mistakes or sins. Growing up, I was often labeled a "hot fast girl" by adults. However, I realized that such treatment wasn't godly. The guilt, shame, and remorse weighed heavily on me. In a moment of despair, I turned to Romans 8:1-39. Delving into this scripture initiated a transformative process within me. My main objective became to heal the 16-year-old inside me, seeking solace. While I'd always been a dependable support for others, I hadn't taken the time to heal and forgive myself. Rather than solely focusing on rectifying past wrongs, I realized the importance of prioritizing my well-being and moving beyond my pain.

It was a pivotal moment when I gathered the courage to face my past self, specifically the sixteen-year-old Chalissa Houston, in the reflection of a mirror. With deep sincerity, I spoke words of liberation, acknowledging the lessons she provided and expressing gratitude for her presence during that phase of my life. However, it was time to say goodbye to that version of myself. I expressed regret for not allowing myself to recognize and work through the pain, damage, and low self-esteem that affected me. I realized I had moved beyond that girl and committed myself to a journey of healing my soul, mind, and heart.

In the name of Jesus, I let go of the past, inviting tranquility to envelop me. I longed to lead a life free from the weight of yesteryears, driven to evolve into the woman I dreamed of becoming, unchained from anything that restricted me. Each day, I implored God to take residence in my heart, seeking His protection and guidance. Surrendering myself to His divine presence, I welcomed Him to assume His rightful position within me. Through this act, I aimed to dismantle the barriers of fear and defeat that had entrenched themselves in my psyche, invoking Jesus's name to channel His strength and bestow upon me liberation.

In wrapping up, my life as Chalissa Houston stands as a testament to determination, tenacity, and a profound drive to effect positive change. From my early days surrounded by family affection to my quest for education and spiritual growth, I've consistently aimed to surmount hurdles and fulfill my aspirations. As a healthcare professional, my successes weren't confined to my vocation alone but extended to the establishment of nurturing daycare environments where children receive the affection and backing they rightly deserve. This steadfast commitment to their welfare and learning underscores both my compassionate nature and my vision of sculpting a brighter tomorrow for the upcoming generation.

I aspire for my narrative to inspire others, signifying that with grit and unwavering resolve, they too can surmount difficulties and craft a purposeful existence. My journey underscores the potency of faith, love, and the significance of chasing dreams, even when adversity looms large. Through my notable achievements and persistent dedication, I symbolize the transformative might of diligence, fortitude, and a relentless aim to positively influence the lives of many.

Acknowledgements

First and foremost, I would like to express my deepest gratitude to Jehovah Rapha, for it is through His unwavering presence and guidance that I have managed to preserve my sanity during even the most tumultuous and dysfunctional times of my life. His divine intervention has provided me with the strength and resilience to navigate through the darkest of storms, and for that, I am eternally grateful.

In addition to relying on Jehovah Rapha's steadfastness, I have found solace and inspiration in the daily reading of Scripture. Each day, without fail, I immerse myself in the sacred verses that nourish my soul and grant me a sense of purpose and hope. Among the passages that have profoundly impacted my life, Romans 8:28 stands as a beacon of light and reassurance. It reminds me that, despite the trials and tribulations that may come my way, all things work together for the good of those who love God—a comforting reminder that even in the midst of chaos, there is a higher plan at play.

By opening up about my own struggles and triumphs, I aspire to ignite a sense of empowerment within others. I want them to know that they are not alone in their struggles and that it is indeed possible to overcome even the darkest days of life. Through resilience, faith, and a steadfast belief in one's ability to persevere, one can emerge from the depths of despair stronger and more resilient than ever before.

Daily Bible Verses

Romans 8: 1-2
[1] Therefore, there is now no condemnation for those who are in Christ Jesus,
[2] because through Christ Jesus the law of the Spirit who gives life has set you free from the law of sin and death.

Proverbs 4:23
"Above all else, guard your heart, for everything you do flows from it."

Romans 8:28
"And we know that in all things God works for the good of those who love him, who have been called according to his purpose."

GRACEFULLY SURVIVED

MARCELINE WILLIAMS

Ordained, Appointed and anointed to pray for the Leaders. Born to Apostle Doris Grant Young and Byron Wiley, and the Great-Great Granddaughter of African Methodist Episcopal Church Bishop, Abraham Grant. Answered the call of ministry March 26, 2000 Ordained as an Evangelist under the leadership of Apostle Doris Grant Young in 2002 and appointed the position of Assistant Pastor in the year of 2002. Under the direction of the anointing in Apostle Prophet Jones, the Prophetic gift was released and nurtured. The calling and separation to God's mandate ordered Marceline to relocate to further gain teaching of the Deliverance, Intercession and Prophetic anointing that she moved membership to World Overcomers Outreach Ministry Under Apostle Alton R. Williams.

Licensed by Apostle Alton R. Williams 2011 as a Minister of the Gospel and other certifications as follows: Apostolic Harvest Leader, Deliverance, Prayer, Prophetic, Teaching and Evangelism. 2012 she launched Prayer Garden of Memphis, ministry called to bridge the gap among denominations and Pastors to pray together in the communities, cities, states and Nation that prayer will bring change when in agreement and partnership, birthed through prayer at World Overcomers Outreach Ministry Church. Intercessory Prayer frontline training and Prophetic training by Apostle Almenthia McCray Foster, Church on the Rock. The love of Christ is her mandate to break the lost free from bondage, and bring order, direction and reconciliation to pursue God's ordained purpose for one's life. Currently Marceline is the intercessory prayer leader at The Pursuit of God Transformation Center where Pastors are Ricky Floyd and Sheila Floyd. The co-author of Tying the Knot between Ministry and the MarketPlace, Annual Event Host (The Annual Day of Prayer, Praise and Healing) (Pastoral Gathering were 24 prayers are prayer by Pastors), 24 Hour Prayer launched in September 2019 in Memphis, TN under the partnership of Pastor Ricky and Sheila Floyd, and most recent book to be published, "On The Wall" The Intercessors Break-Threw Prayer. Prayer Garden of Memphis merged with The Pursuit of God Transformation Center in 2018. She is a doctoral Candidate at Ashford University, and holds an MBA at Belhaven Christian University.

Provided upon request: Ministry Prayer Trainings
Altar Trainings
Strategy to Develop Prayer Teams
Establishing Prayer in the Church
Kingdom Vision to Manifestation

GRACEFULLY SURVIVED

The sky is clear and blue, and the time now is around 2:00 pm in the late fall, but this started the beginning of Spring. "Little girl, where is your mother and why are you here? Go home and stay from this area"! It was in the outside area where fun and friendly children would be playing, however inside the house was darkness, wickedness, and manipulative voices all around. Who would have known that the house filled with laughing children, a mother, a father, and other family members next door would experience so much trauma.

Day after day, week after week, month after month and year after year, toddlers and young girls and boys experience sexual abuse, mental abuse, and trauma from abuse at the hands of family members. However, family kept secrets causes generations of the inherited blood line to continue to be harmed and maliciously abused to protect a name. Here's little Mary's story. One day it was discovered that it was time for little Mary's monthly menstrual cycle to start. It came out of nowhere. The people in the house were saying, "somebody go to the store and get some pads". Mary was so confused and was left wondering what was happening because no one told her about what to do when starting her cycle. She was unprepared. Meanwhile, she is bleeding and still confused about how to stop it or when it will stop. So she sat in the bathroom until someone came in with a Kotex maxi pad (for adults) and said, "Okay, remove the sticker and place it inside your underwear, this will catch the blood". Mary did exactly what she was told.

Despite this unfortunate experience, most of the time Mary was timid and shy, with no street sense and all curiosity. Playing and running up and down the streets of Smoky City, while going to school and church because there were two things Mary's aunt did not play about . . . that was school and church. You could hear her Auntie shouting, "You better get up and get ready", for school or church depending on the day. This included attending every week of Vacation Bible School. This sounds like a typical little girl's childhood with happiness and laughter. Then it all changed when it was time to move next door to the other side of the family.

Oftentimes, those who have been abused may not recall exactly when and how they may be abused. This form of memory loss or suppression, tends to be a commonality amongst those who have been abused. These were the same thoughts and gestures as for little Mary. Mary first became aware of one of her gifts at the age of nine. She did not fully understand it but she would wake in the middle of the night and quote scriptures and preach. Mary asked her mom what was wrong with her. She wanted answers because little Mary did not know her biological father, only the other men that would one day be known as the "*perpetrators*" from the age of eleven until sixteen in the midst of three different households. Without giving an explanation, Little Mary's mom told her, "oh child someday you will know".

> So, what is a perpetrator—*a person who carries out a harmful, illegal, or immoral act*
>
> (Oxford Dictionary).

Early Spring arrived, trees were green, flowers were blooming and it was time for Little Mary's birthday. She was so happy and excited, just to see her birthday, because she never remembered having cake, ice cream or even a party, but she always received a pack of gum. This made her wonder if someone was trying to say her breath stink or just playing tricks. She was happy to be turning eleven years old. It appeared the unexpected first perpetrator must have been waiting on that day because it was during this time they showed up. For Mary, it was so vague in memory as she tried to erase it, but it never left her conscious. She would never forget because one day her perpetrator may encounter more children and Little Mary wanted to protect them.

So, this is what happened. Little Mary said, "Please what are you doing"? The perpetrator responded, "This will be fine. I just want you to lay down and don't move". Mary said, "No, what are you doing"? He said again, "Lay down and don't move". So, what did little Mary do? Little Mary laid down and did not move and suddenly, the perpetrator began. Yes, this was the first time anyone had ever actually taken their male counterpart and placed it upon little Mary's privacy area. Little Mary felt ashamed, betrayed and most of all little Mary felt nasty and dirty.

All she wanted to do was run and tell somebody, but little Mary was reminded of the perpetrator's words, saying "if you tell anybody they are not going to like you no more and they are not going to believe you, so you just as well be quiet". So what happened the next day? The same thing happened again the next day, the next day, and many times after. Little Mary could not figure out why in the world was this perpetrator messing with her. It was not right. Because Mary knew it was not right, little Mary suddenly would ask family if she could go to work with them. Unaware of what had been going on, they would say "no" and she would be left.

In fact, everyone had to go outside and play except little Mary and she would be forced to do things that a child should not know or ever must do. If you haven't gotten it by now, yes little Mary's innocence was taken.

One night when the perpetrator took a shower, they came into little Mary's room and at that time had proceeded to do it again when suddenly, a family member came in the room as well. That was the first time that the perpetrator was caught and confronted. Little Mary was sick because no one believed her when she admitted that this had been going on for at least six months without anyone noticing or stopping it. Shortly after the perpetrator was caught, little Mary attended Rape Crisis and confirmed that rape had taken place over several times and had cried every day due to the trauma. By this time little Mary met her biological father and he decided it was best for little Mary to come live with him and his family. This did not go over well with Mary's immediate family. They were upset and tried to convince Mary that her father had not done anything for her but if she wanted to go, then she was free to go. By now, little Mary was 13 years old and starting a new life with her biological father, other siblings, paternal grandparents, uncle and aunt.

This new life gave a brand-new perspective as little Mary was about 5'4" and weighing about 115 pounds. While attending a diverse school she ended up meeting who would be her first boyfriend. Big David was so nice and seemed to understand Mary. This is when the cycle began of being attracted to older men. Yes, Big David was a senior in high school and Mary was a freshman. The age difference was 18 and 14. Mary shared everything with David about her trauma and how she had come to live with her father. Then one day Mary decided to go ahead and have an intimate relationship with Big David. This would be the time she started to believe that this is what was needed to have a man; to do whatever they wanted you to do. Well, Mary got pregnant. Now, thinking the only option was to have an abortion. You see, Mary's mom was pregnant with her at 14 and did not have an abortion. However, Mary's father, aunt, and uncle told her that it was something she should do and by keeping the baby, she would ruin her life. In Memphis there was an abortion clinic on Poplar. It was a two-story house that is still there. Mary listened to her family. Thank God He forgives and heals. Shortly after the abortion, Big David and Mary broke up. Mary was devastated. What had she done to deserve so much turmoil, pain and disappointment. She had the hardest time forgiving herself until she found out that her mother knew all along.

This gave her some comfort knowing that she was not angry with her. However, Mary's aunt reminded Mary's mom that it was not an option to abort Mary. This is why Mary is here today.

Little Mary was determined when she did have children, they would not become pregnant as a teenager or be violated. Go figure, one of the two was not prevented. For one thing, people did not realize that little Mary was all by herself without anyone to protect her. She had no one praying for her or encouraging her, so she thought, until it was discovered later in her life that she did have a praying aunt.

Mary continued to live with her father and life was pretty good. I guess you could consider them as a middle class family because her father worked for a well-known factory, her grandfather worked for the only utility company, her aunt worked for a major department store and her uncle had his own business. It was totally different from living with her mom where from the looks of the neighborhood and old house, one might assume they were living in poverty. Then, it starts again with other family members and neighbors, Mary was terrified.

Here we go again. It all started with the neighbor as Mary started receiving money for allowance of good report cards. Then all of a sudden the perpetrators would attempt to feel Mary breast and posterior. It is so important that all parents and family members be very watchful of children even around other family and friends you may know very well. Because Mary was not being watched, she continued to get caught up in situations no child should be in. For instance, the neighbor would say, "I got $20 for you Mary if you let me feel your breast" and Mary would allow it. That particular act would go on for at least a year. It was so bad, Mary began to think that people were saying she was no good. Sometimes, Mary thought she might agree. One might ask, what if little Mary never had her innocence taken.

How different would her life have been? What choices would she have made? Personally, I believe little Mary was at a point where she no longer cared about where her life was heading or the choices she was making because no one cared for her. At this point, she was emotionally disconnected from men. She had been used and abused and now she was tired.

So, who is little Mary now? You should know by now that it is I. No longer little Mary . . . just Mary. Yes, that 5'4" inch 115 pound, bright eyed girl had a heart that was empty and a brain that was aimed to manipulate and to control. Some people may not admit that. Now I am 16 years old when I am introduced to more bad habits. This time, I am introduced to marijuana, crack, hash and alcohol. I was being molested again by another family member but this time when I told the family they believed me and it stopped. I started dating another older man that was seven years older than me and for my 16th birthday was the first time I literally got drunk too much alcohol. I was to the point that he had to carry me in the house to my father. At that point my dad did not like him anymore. We stopped dating but we did remain friends. Shortly after, I moved on to a new boyfriend who was three years older than me. He was so sweet. Up to that point, he was probably the best guy that I had ever met. It always seemed as if I was important to him. In fact we were still together until I decided to marry someone else. So why didn't Mary marry him? Big D, as I will call him, was so insecure we would fight continuously all the time, but big D is the one that made me a mother after two miscarriages. I had my first successful pregnancy with him. Each time I would get pregnant, within 6 to 8 weeks I would lose the baby mostly due to stress. I believe my unhappiness and not really taking care of myself might have had something to do with it as well. One of my greatest memories of my relationship with Big D is when he proposed to me on my prom night. He not only proposed but he took care of everything for my senior prom. He always spoiled me, but being spoiled came along with arguing and fighting. This relationship would be my first encounter of domestic violence.

It was actually around 12 years old when I met Big D. I was crazy about this chubby guy when we actually lived down the street from one another. I would go down the street and his mom would tell him I was there to see him. He would say he didn't want to see me and he wanted me to go home. No one could have known that one day Big D would be as crazy about me as I was about him then. We ended up seeing each other again when I was around 16 years old and yes, I had changed and so had he. The changes that took place during our relationship was not OK. Like I said before, this was my first encounter with domestic violence. The very first physical altercation was when big D came to my father's house and saw me getting out of the car with someone else. I could barely walk up the driveway before he was right behind me. That's when the first smack to my cheek took place. At that point my father came outside and pulled him off me. Not too much time passed before he came back with the right words I thought I wanted to hear. I continued to date him even after my father said I wasn't allowed. So, from age 16 to 20, I was still dating this man and subjecting myself to domestic violence. I will never forget we had a fight so bad while we were at his parents' home. We were upstairs. His mother had come upstairs because she heard us fighting and said we needed to stop. It had been going far too long when she pulled me off of him and him off of me. At that moment I told myself it was over. I couldn't do it anymore. Well yet again it was not over. Since we continued to date, we also continued to be intimate. As I said before we had two miscarriages. I finally was able to hold a baby and successfully deliver a baby girl which is my oldest today. She was the most beautiful "red" baby weighing 7 pounds three ounces. Shortly after I started dating another man 16 years senior to me. This was the second time domestic violence struck again.

This man would also cause pain physically more than anything else. However, my next three children would come from him. All of my children are my greatest joy and I love each one of them dearly. Now, remember earlier when I was talking about two miscarriages from Big D and how we finally had a baby. I also mentioned that she was red. For this reason, I automatically assumed the man I was with after Big D was the father. Boy, was I wrong. My mother always said Big D was always the father, but I denied it. My mom knew. I left Big D to be with who I thought was the baby's father. I admit, I was no SAINT.

Relationships were not good for me and I wasn't any better with marriage. My husband cherished me, and I thought loved me. So now here we have a man who is 36 years old and this woman Mary who is 20 years old. And another insecure man! This time he was my husband. Why was it hard for him to believe that his woman was faithful? I can recall one day my coworker dropped me off at home. He was standing in the door waiting to see who was bringing me home. Before you knew it, he came out the door and was hollering and screaming telling the person to never bring me home and never let him see me with them again. It was a friendly ride.

It was evident that he had a lot of built-up anger but never understood why. I do know that he never had a relationship with his father. To this day, I believe that played a big part. Next came babies two, and three with this man all within five years. It seemed like I was getting pregnant right after having a baby. And yes, we were still arguing and fighting. When things really hit me, it happened one day during one of our fights. He was choking me over the fireplace and my daughter was coming down the hallway. She saw us and literally stood in the middle of the floor. She started shaking uncontrollably and that was when I found the strength to get away from him to embrace her. I knew in that moment something had to change. I decided right then and there, it was time to leave.

Although the marriage lasted 11 years, we were only together the first five years and the last three years of his life. Eight years total. He always said he did not want a divorce and he would not file. I filed for divorce three times. After the third filing the attorney passed away before anything took place.

Separated from my husband, I have now found real love, joy, and peace. I am in a relationship with my Savior Jesus Christ, and he is Lord of my life. This is the best relationship I could ever have. Under the leadership of King Jesus, I heard to stop pursuing the divorce. I obeyed the voice of the Lord and six months later I received a phone call from a friend that said my husband was sick. I stepped back into his life taking the place of his wife. Right where he needed me. I nurtured and consoled him, doing everything I could until he took his last breath. I asked him for forgiveness. I also asked him to accept Jesus Christ as his Lord and Savior. I even thanked him for the children that were a blessing as a result of our union. God is amazing. He shows us the principles of a godly man and it is up to us as women to watch and look for those principles in any man that we date or investigate as marriage. It is true if you see the red flags up front do not ignore them. I can't stress that enough because I was still searching for someone to love me instead of letting a godly man find me. As a result, I fell into another relationship, and it ended up being one of the worst traumas of my life thus far.

God's goodness showed during my husband's battle with the big C. Yes, that big C, you know the one. He was really sick, and even ended up on a ventilator. Everyone kept saying, "Let him go, take him off." But whether it was peace or just plain lack of strength on my part, I couldn't. Twelve weeks on that machine, and by some miracle – God's grace I'd say – he came off it. Lived another two years. That was God showing us he's a healer. Now with him gone, I've got these four kids to think about. Decisions aren't easy. If another man were to come into our lives, would he love them like I do? And not just three of them; all four. They deserve a father's love, right?

Then, as if life wasn't testing me enough, the kids' uncle – the man I thought would step up as a male figure for them – passed too, just nine months after their dad.

And guess what? The big C got him as well. To me, this big C started feeling like a spider web, sneaking in, taking away all that's good. It was winter when we were burying their father. Cold times, hard times. I won't lie; it broke me seeing my kids crying daily. Despite everything – and believe me, we've been through a lot, even thought of divorce – I know he loved those kids. I think he loved me too. But is love enough to stick through a relationship that's unhappy, even abusive? I just want what's best: happiness, love, and maybe someone who understands God's plan for us.

Here we go again thinking, "this has to be truly the best thing that has happened". Well that's what I thought right. I was so wrong again. Here I am, living righteously, trying to be a God-fearing woman, now left as a widow with four small children. I think I've got 7-year-old twins, a 9-year-old, and an 11-year-old. But then again, maybe they were 6-year-old twins, an 8-year-old, and a 10-year-old. You get the point. They're young.

Abuse can leave one heartless, vulnerable, with low self-esteem. It can even cause you to be on guard, over-protective, and defensive. Even then, sometimes you can miss the mark. Working in corporate America and more specifically in law enforcement, I met the perpetrator that caused the very pain that I promised my children would not encounter. This was so devastating because the person I let in appeared to be loving, compassionate, and sympathetic as well as showed empathy for everything that I had experienced and been through. I was so upset and mad at myself until I literally lost my mental capacity to think that I was ever worth anything because of the bad choice I had made. Totally blinded by the outcome of this relationship, it left me bitter and heartless. How could I make this mistake, and not discern what this truly was. Here it is, a little girl confiding in this person, just like sitting on daddy's lap, simply because it was another older man. Betrayal and deception were the attributes received because I thought this was the blessing finally reaching me after all that had been encountered. Did I see this coming?

No. Little Mary had failed to protect her precious baby just like someone failed to protect her. Never, never is it the child's fault. Statements such as, "that girl was fast", "she should have put some clothes on", or "she is having sex anyway" is no justification for sexual abuse. It is unfortunate when a mother does not listen to a daughter and other children are molested or raped at the hand of the same person because the parent didn't act on behalf of the child. The parent didn't ensure that the perpetrator was removed or better yet everyone involved sought counseling or therapy.

Trauma that is not addressed can show up as anger, then anger becomes rage, rage becomes hatred, hatred all combined can result in murder which is death. This is why we have to share our stories. To help others. A woman who has been molested can connect with another woman who has had the same or similar experience with the mission to prevent another boy or girl from going through the same thing. This is why. I heard a man that molested a child say, "women need to get over that because it will never stop". We have to normalize the conversation around inappropriate touching and empower our children to share when someone is approaching them in inappropriate ways and children must know what is inappropriate. As parents, we have to pay more attention to our children and who they spend time with. Here's a scenario to think about. Imagine a home with a mother, father and maybe four children (2 girls and 2 boys). Every day the children tell the mother, when they get home the daddy goes into the room with Sally or Bob and the door is locked. What does the mother do? It's sad to say but this is one example of many where sexual abuse is taking place right in the home and goes unaddressed for various reasons. Sometimes the children may not directly say what's going on depending on the age of the child and because they just don't know, parents can ask more questions and investigate the matter for themselves.

Focusing on the outcome and the damage as a result of sexual trauma has left some women permanently incapable of bearing their own children. Unfortunately, some have decided not to have any because of the childhood trauma they experienced.

Surely, they don't want to see their children experience the same actions, and some place guilt on themselves and feel it's because of their sins. Was it supposed to happen? No, it was not. After all I went through, it was consistent prayer and a true relationship with God, with my faith of believing in Jesus Christ that gave me strength to **Gracefully Survive** in my mind as he restored my heart and gave me the power to forgive. I now walk boldly in the love of God and knowing that all things work together for my good, because I know I am called according to His purpose (that nine-year-old waking up preaching) and I love Him wholeheartedly Romans 8:28. Little Mary, now Mary is not her mother or her father, she is an individual and she chooses to live abundantly and in the favor of the Lord. The healing process was not overnight, but Mary never gave up. Being a successful owner of three businesses, having amazing and successful children, and mentees that Mary prays for and encourages often keeps her in the perfect will of God. The wrong prey may find one such as Mary but with prayer, they will not keep her and this, which is called discernment, will work every time. The pain can be cured, not just halfway but all the way, and those that have been shattered from their innocence being taken, not given, must believe and embrace that wholeness. Mary took a survey of the women in a family known by her about sexual abuse. The results of this survey showed thirteen out of sixteen girls and women in the room had been molested by another family member or friend of a family member. This completely says there is a generational curse from sexual demons influencing that bloodline. Ask yourself will you be one to help stop the spread of hurting little girls and little boys? Silence is not okay and I will continue to advocate until an action is distinguished and our children are safe.

Children that have been sexually molested go through many changes until they can be delivered, healed and set free. Most importantly, they have to build up their self-esteem and believe that they have purpose. Traveling down this memory lane has really brought old wounds back to life, so in the name of Jesus I pray that the transparency and the authenticity of what has been written will be an eye opener for other women. Also, I pray strength is ignited the moment that any woman or man which has come through trauma, sexual abuse, verbal abuse, mental abuse, physical abuse, domestic violence or self-abuse reads these stories and as tears run, you forgive and heal. Live life abundantly and wholeheartedly in love.

Gracefully Survived

Important Information About Sexual Abuse https://www.earlyopenoften. org/get-the-facts/signs-of-sexual-abuse/

- Acting younger or going back to doing younger tasks and activities
- Sudden changes in behavior
- Fear of being alone with a certain person
- Sudden, unexplained fears of certain places or kinds of people (such as all people with a particular feature or characteristic)
- Fear of being touched.
- Changes in quality of schoolwork or grades

- Substance abuse
- Delinquency
- Self-mutilation or careless behaviors resulting in self-harm.
- Excessive play with their own private body parts
- Persistent sex play with friends, toys, or pets
- Frequent drawings that have sexual content
- Unusual, persistent, or developmentally inappropriate questioning about human sexuality

These changes might not be dramatic but could include several subtle changes. It's important to know what's natural and healthy in <u>kids' sexual development</u> (for example, many young children are curious about sexuality and frequently play with their private body parts). Knowing these stages of development will help you notice if something doesn't seem right, which might indicate a problem.

Physical Signs

These are some physical signs that could indicate a problem, including the possibility of sexual abuse:

- Eating more or less than usual
- Having trouble sleeping
- Soiling or wetting clothes, or bedwetting (or an increase, if it happens already)
- Stomach aches
- Physical pain or itching in the genital area.
- Underwear stained with blood or other discharge.
- Rectal bleeding
- Problems walking or sitting.

If your child shows any of the physical signs listed above, take him or her to a doctor right away.

Emotional Signs

These are some emotional signs that could indicate a problem, including the possibility of sexual abuse:

- Severe anxiety (such as nightmares or clinging)
- Depression (such as withdrawal, low self-esteem, thinking about or attempting suicide, or frequent crying)
- Extreme anger (for example, tantrums, aggression, or increased irritability) Talk to your doctor or the counselor at your child's school if your child shows any of these emotional signs.

This book shall impact many, if not 1,000,000, encouraging them to tell their side of the story. It's time we alert the sexual offenders and perpetrators, serving them and the enemy notice that they did not and cannot stop the **Plans of God**.

www.ingramcontent.com/pod-product-compliance
Lightning Source LLC
Chambersburg PA
CBHW071425150726
48000CB00001B/477